Matt,

Thank you for hosting such
an amazing podcast and for
your continued support!

Keep in touch.

Randy Keirnan

A LOGICAL APPROACH

to

SPIRITUALITY

Shattering The Religious Paradigm
And Finding Your Inner Truth

RANDY KLEINMAN

Publishing Services provided by Paper Raven Books

Printed in the United States of America

First Printing, 2021

Paperback ISBN= 978-1-7367134-0-2
Hardback ISBN= 978-1-7367134-1-9

To Alana—thank you for your continuous inspiration and support

TABLE OF CONTENTS

"For my ally is the Force, and a powerful ally it is. Life creates it, makes it grow. Its energy surrounds us and binds us. Luminous beings are we, not this crude matter. You must feel the Force around you; here, between you, me, the tree, the rock, everywhere, yes."

—Yoda

INTRODUCTION

If you picked up this book, it was not an accident. As we will later discuss, I believe that very few things in life are.

So, why did you open this book?

Maybe it's because you are one of the many people who consider themselves to be spiritual but reject the idea of having an official religious affiliation.

Maybe you are uncertain what your particular spiritual beliefs are, but you know that you're fed up with the hypocrisy that has become almost synonymous with many mainstream religions.

Maybe you feel conflicted. On the one hand, you see that spirituality has the potential to add value to your life. You know that you believe in *something*, but you're just not sure how to articulate it. On the other hand, you reject the dogmatic principles and archaic traditions perpetuated by most religions.

Or maybe it was just the catchy title and pretty cover that caught your attention.

Whatever your specific motivation was, I understand. At first glance, you probably wouldn't expect that I'd be someone who would be interested in spirituality, let alone write an entire book on the subject. Most days, I wear a suit for my job as a lawyer at a boutique law firm in New York. Some days, you can find me arguing in court or talking to a jury. Other days, you can find me sitting behind a desk and pumping out motions. But the more I did this, the more I realized that I was really just going *through* the motions. There was no real passion. No real love.

I used to feel like there was an entirely different person living inside of me, underneath the surface, hiding in fear. I was afraid of being judged. I was afraid that people would recognize my imperfections and call me a fraud, a phony, a hypocrite. I allowed only those closest to me to ever see my true self. I was extremely guarded.

Does this sound familiar to you?

I was just like you. Something was missing in my spiritual life. I feel like people have always tried to tell me how I should think. What's right. What's wrong. What's possible. What's impossible. But I could never just truly accept that. Some people call it an authority problem; however, I think it's something much deeper than that. I don't have a problem with authority. I have a problem with conformity. I have a problem with the status quo. I have a problem with groupthink, with being confined, with having my creativity suppressed.

Feeling this way led me on an eighteen-year journey of dedicated study, during which I have been fully immersed in literature on spirituality and metaphysics and am now fully embedded into the spiritual community. I am constantly researching and reading new books, articles, and blogs; listening to podcasts; watching documentaries; attending online workshops; or thinking about spirituality. I have also studied many different religions both during and after college and was effectively a religious studies minor. This has taken me down many rabbit holes (and maybe even some wormholes) and has opened my mind to an infinite range of possibilities.

What makes this book different from others is that I'm just an ordinary person. I'm not a "spiritual guru," I am not "enlightened," and I am certainly not perfect. I have made—and continue to make—many mistakes. I have vices. Simply stated, I am magnificently, wonderfully, and innately flawed. But, while I make many mistakes, I try to learn from them. I am continuously seeking to grow spiritually. I, like you, am simply a student of this great planet. I am unmistakably and spectacularly human.

Together, we will explore the paranormal, esoteric, and abstract—the mystical, magical, and unseen phenomena that shape our world. The things that are seemingly beyond our reach and control. If nothing else, I want to make spirituality more accessible to everyone who reads this by encouraging open and honest discourse about its relationship with our everyday lives. Thus, I envision this as your portal into spirituality and a pathway toward spiritual growth. I hope to help fill a spiritual void while leaving you with a desire to keep exploring.

CHAPTER 1

AN INTRODUCTION TO SPIRITUALITY

Our society is on the precipice of a cultural revolution. The religious hegemonies are crumbling, and many of us are beginning to reject the draconian sociopolitical archetypes that have created the existing paradigms, paving the way for a new approach to spirituality. There is a palpable tension that's hard to define. It lingers. It's so pervasive that you can almost taste it.

Our society is angry. We are awakening to massive inequities that have plagued our planet for millennia and are rightfully demanding that justice be served. But in our earnest attempt to safeguard equality and despite our good intentions, we have become more reactive than logical. Instead of encouraging proactive discourse, we have begun to suppress the opinions of those who do not share in our own ideals. This has created echo chambers where only those ideas that mirror our own are reflected. Instead of looking for solutions internally, we blame outside forces.

But as we will discuss, a spiritual approach requires that we first recognize our oneness with all other things and then look within ourselves for a solution. If we are going to build a utopian society, we must encourage everyone to speak and live their truth. It is only through candid and logical dialogue that we can catalyze our spiritual growth and cultural revolution into a spiritual renaissance!

My Intentions

The purpose of this book is to provide an eclectic overview of spirituality and demonstrate how seemingly esoteric subjects are supported by modern science and common sense. The ideas contained in this book are predicated on a principle called the Law of One, which states that all things—all of life and creation—are part of one original thought. That we are unified by a singular consciousness. Together, we will explore the science behind this principle and discuss how we can use this concept to recognize our oneness with all other things and live more loving lives. I believe this ideology can help our society overcome the polarizing issues that unfortunately dominate the sociopolitical landscape and have managed to permeate nearly every aspect of our everyday lives. In so doing, we can spread light, love, and awaken souls globally.

One of my goals is to make spirituality more relatable by approaching it practically, logically, and from the casual perspective of a layperson. My hope is that this sparks a flame inside you that resonates and inspires a desire for spiritual growth. I want to show you that spirituality is open to interpretation and not a one-size-fits-all formula like religion. The odds are that if you are reading this book, you have probably already started your journey and are beginning to awaken and reject the archaic religious paradigms that have controlled the spiritual narrative for millennia. You probably agree that our society is ready for new ideas that explain how we can be spiritual, empathetic, and compassionate beings without conforming to the arbitrary—and often superstitious—religious customs that most of us simply inherited at birth.

I have done my best to make this book accessible to everyone, regardless of their race, religion, gender, ethnicity, or age. If you already consider yourself to be spiritually "awakened," I hope this book can offer new and interesting insights into your established belief system and help further your spiritual journey. If you feel lost, uncertain, or confused, I hope this book can provide some clarity and inspire you to unlock your true spiritual potential. If you're simply curious, I hope you find these concepts stimulating and engaging. Either way, I hope that we can all open our minds to the possibility that our existence in this world has far greater significance than what we can perceive with our limited physical senses. Nothing is arbitrary.

I'd like to be clear at the very beginning that this is not a step-by-step guide to attaining absolute spiritual enlightenment. Nor am I qualified to provide such instruction. Anyone claiming to do so should be viewed with a measure of skepticism. Besides, I always find that the extremes inherent in step-by-step guides to "absolute" anything are far too rigorous to offer any sustainable value. The pursuit of "absolute" spiritual enlightenment, although admirable, would require a level of commitment that is simply not realistic for most. Very few of us would be willing to sacrifice our families, friends, careers, and passions to pursue this goal.

That said, two main points are worth emphasizing as the most important aspects of this book. The first is that spirituality can be unique to each of us. You don't need me, or anyone else, to tell you what you should believe and how you should think. I think we can all agree that there's already enough of that going around these days. While I'll certainly offer my opinion and some suggestions along the way, nothing I say is absolute. The second is that, although nothing I say is absolute, the central aspect of my spiritual belief system is founded on the principle that, in its simplest form, *all things are one*. We will explore this idea in more detail throughout the book.

Here's all that I ask from you: as you read this book, please try to create your version of spirituality. Spirituality should be as personal to you as your identity. It can be simple. It can be complex. It can be whatever you want it to be. Just make sure that it's yours. In the end, the purpose of spirituality is to help *you* get through life.

So, when I discuss my spiritual beliefs, you should put your spin on them. The ideas in this book are just ideas, and my role here is like a tour guide who leads the way through stimulating, rugged, and unexplored terrain. This job requires that I brush aside the tall grass for you to see the beautiful landscapes and architecture that will help you paint the perfect portrait of your ever-evolving belief system. Indeed, the emphasis on individuality is at the core of spiritual practice and is a big part of what separates spirituality from religion. This is why I'll never tell you what to think. Instead, I encourage you to let your intuition guide you to your version of the truth. Pick and choose what you want to take away. Add to them; criticize them; love them; hate them. You make the rules. This is spirituality *a la carte!*

Because spirituality involves every aspect of our lives, I'll be sharing some stories about my own life to help provide context. I'll also draw some analogies from pop culture. In essence, this book is really partly spiritual, partly philosophical, partly social commentary, and partly common sense. I don't expect you to agree with everything I say. But what I do hope is that I can offer an interesting perspective on life and our purpose as both individuals and as a species. Because we will be discussing deeply personal and vulnerable topics, you might find yourself triggered by something I've said. That's absolutely okay! Everyone's life experiences and outlooks differ. If you find that this has happened while you're reading, you might find it helpful to remember my central belief that we are all *one* and to utilize this as the opportunity to tailor your unique spiritual perspective.

A lot of what I discuss falls under the category of metaphysics. Some of you may already be familiar with this term, but it's really just a fancy way of saying "spiritual philosophy" or "spiritualism." Metaphysics explores the fundamental nature of reality, existence, and experience without any singular theological doctrine. Metaphysics is spirituality without religion and dogma.[1] Metaphysics is the study of the universe, the soul, and the physical and nonphysical realms. Metaphysics explores the idea that our ultimate reality is actually spiritual. Again, I am not trying to convince you of anything. Nor do I intend for anything I say to be taken as gospel. I encourage each of you to question these concepts and explore them further.

Another reason I wrote this book is to demonstrate that science and spirituality are not mutually exclusive, but rather complementary. When you read as much about spirituality as I do, you see words like "miracle" and "God" a lot. But what you don't often see is any tangible proof that these things actually exist. Of course, it's pretty hard to prove any of these things because they can't really be seen, measured, or touched. The expectation is that we simply accept these ideas as truth without any type of proof.

Nor does spirituality have to be an all-or-nothing proposition. We shouldn't have to sacrifice all of life's pleasures to achieve some level of spiritual enlightenment. After all, it's these very pleasures that provide us with the most joy and are critical to our happiness. If we were to eliminate our basic pleasures, we would diminish our potential to appreciate life. This is counterproductive to our happiness and spiritual development. This is not to say that we shouldn't strike a balance between pleasure and our physical and spiritual health. But we must embrace our passions and live our lives to the fullest potential every moment. The point is that it is very difficult to sustain an extreme, all-or-nothing lifestyle. Hence, the cliché: everything in moderation. But spirituality and happiness should not be mutually exclusive concepts.

As I alluded to earlier, spirituality can be an incredibly dense subject. It encompasses so many different things that this book will merely scratch the surface. I don't intend to provide a comprehensive overview on any one spiritual, scientific, or religious topic. Instead, my goal is really to provide you with a basic overview of spirituality and demonstrate how it can affect our lives in ways you may never have even considered. Perhaps we can explore these topics more thoroughly in future books. But if I tried to do that here, I'd either never have finished this book or it would be so long that you'd never want to read it. So, if you find yourself asking questions about certain things that I may not have covered, let's continue the conversation! Connect with me through email at randyEkleinman@gmail.com. Please, just reach out!

What We Will Cover

Now that I've explained my intentions and provided some insight, I'd like to walk you through what we're going to cover.

In chapter 2, I briefly discuss my religious upbringing and how this turned me away from organized religion and helped to shape my spiritual perspective. In chapter 3, we will dive into the theory of oneness and talk about finding our true spiritual essence by breaking through years of social conditioning. We then begin exploring the historical tension between religion and science in chapter 4. We will also take a look at how the theory of oneness suggests that humanity shares in a collective consciousness and how this idea has been supported by scientists like Albert Einstein and Carl Jung. Chapter 5 takes a closer look at the Law of One material, what it says about creation, and how this information has been distorted over many thousands of years. This will segue into a conversation about my favorite topic: outer space and the overwhelming evidence of extraterrestrials!

In chapter 6, we will discuss how we can each find and live our spiritual truth. I talk about my struggles with adversity and how I finally found my spiritual path through intuition and honesty. I also discuss how the current culture of outrage is anathema to spirituality and how simply changing our perspective can help us overcome our differences. Chapter 7 describes why spiritual growth requires that we not only forgive others but that we also forgive ourselves. This leads to a discussion about reincarnation and how it fits into the overall spiritual puzzle. Chapter 8 explores how the universe sends us messages through a multitude of synchronistic events and symbols. I'll explain how these synchronicities can help guide you along your spiritual path. Next, in chapter 9, we'll talk about the importance of finding balance in our everyday lives by living a healthy lifestyle both physically through exercise and mentally through meditation and prayer. We will conclude in chapter 10 by discussing how humanities' spiritual progress is cyclical and the need for each of us to choose either a positive or negative spiritual path.

The concepts explored in this book are intended to stimulate your sense of spirituality. Let's work to galvanize this spiritual renaissance by exploring this topic with a fresh perspective, by shedding all pretext and pretense.

CHAPTER 2
A BRIEF RELIGIOUS CRITIQUE

When we think about modern-day religious oppression, most of us probably look to the Middle East. We think about lesser-developed countries whose laws are modeled on religious principles. We think about countries like Saudi Arabia. We probably don't consider our religions to be particularly oppressive.

I think we can all agree that religious oppression is typically relegated to those who practice in the most extreme sects. It's not often that we see this type of oppression in our neighborhoods. But perhaps this is because we're not looking closely enough.

Growing up, I was raised Jewish. We weren't a particularly religious family, but I went to Hebrew school as a kid, attended the occasional weekend service, and liberally observed most of the major holidays with my family. As a child, I accepted Judaism as part of my life because I didn't know anything different. Children are very impressionable, so it's easy for them to accept what they're told without asking too many substantive questions.

But as I got older, I started to question seemingly arbitrary rules and customs and the incredible stories associated with religion. By the time I was in high school, I recognized that most religions were essentially the same at their core. There were some differences, but I really couldn't understand why our society feels so compelled to divide and categorize these religions into separate belief systems. By the time I got to college, I started studying different religions and eventually stumbled across books on metaphysics. In addition to my reading, I took many religion-themed classes, including classes on Judaism, Catholicism, and Asian religions.

This research only solidified my belief that we don't need religion to be spiritual. It also made me much more critical of religion. I learned a lot about Judaism, particularly Hasidic Jewish culture. This is one of the strictest factions of Judaism where every aspect of a person's life is controlled by incredibly complex rules to an authoritarian degree. These rules govern things like how they must wear their hair, how they dress, what they are permitted to eat, and even how and when they are permitted to have sex. It's an incredibly militaristic culture, and each member must strictly follow the rules. Questions are not tolerated. Dissent is punished. Philosophical discussions or debates are entirely prohibited. Freethinking is taboo. It is an incredibly insular community, and its members are forbidden from reading books or even entering a secular library, watching movies, listening to music, or even using the internet.

In college, the Jewish studies courses were taught by a family of Hasidic rabbis, one of whom is a very prominent figure within the Hasidic community. I had an excellent rapport with the rabbis, particularly the eldest son, Avraham.

What I found most perplexing about these courses was how religion and way of living revolved around such circular logic. I would often engage in philosophical debates with the rabbi. Well, debate is probably too strong of a word. It was more like me asking a lot of questions, being frustrated with the answers, and asking more questions. I would challenge the rabbi on many issues, such as the obvious subjugation of women that is seemingly authorized by the so-called Jewish law. The rabbi would always have superficial responses like, "Judaism doesn't subjugate women, it venerates them." According to the rabbi, this is why women are tasked with the most important job of all: taking care of the household and family. The more I challenged the rabbi's response, the more circular his logic became, until he inevitably circled to a response like, "Because this is what God wants."

These answers were never good enough for me. He might as well have just answered all of my questions with the word "because."

The rabbi's answers got dicey when I would challenge him about things like dinosaurs and fossils. One time, I asked him how Judaism reconciles its claim that the Earth is only a few thousand years old with carbon dating that shows rocks and fossils that are hundreds of millions of years old. The rabbi's response was classic.

According to the rabbi, our carbon dating system is flawed as a result of the Great Flood, which distorted the physiology of rocks and fossils, making it seem like they were much older than they are. According to the rabbi, humans inhabited the Earth together with dinosaurs about 5,780 years ago. That's right— even though there is absolutely no historical or scientific evidence of this whatsoever, the rabbi believes that less than 6,000 years ago, dinosaurs were walking around with humans.

Touché, rabbi. How could I possibly argue with this? The rabbi was so committed to Judaism and so determined to perpetuate his way of living (and so brainwashed) that he was willing to overlook objective evidence, logic, and common sense. It's certainly easier to simply believe everything we are told and never ask questions. But this has a chilling effect on progress.

Of course, many religions and cultures operate like this. This is not something unique to Judaism. I just happen to have insight into Jewish culture. If my studies taught me one thing it's that Judaism, in its strictest form, is an oppressive and divisive religion.

When I was in my mid-twenties, I was living in Brooklyn, New York. On a Friday evening in late fall, I had just exited the subway at my stop. It wasn't too late, and the sun was just beginning to set. The subway station let passengers off on a raised outdoor platform. To leave, I had to walk up a set of stairs and exit through a small station house.

As I entered the station house, I saw a Hasidic Jewish teenager, probably around eighteen years old. He was holding a set of papers and frantically approaching people walking by. At first, I wasn't able to hear him, but as I got closer his words became clearer. The man was begging, pleading with passersby to take his stack of papers. He was frantic, on the verge of literal hysterics.

When I finally reached the man, he was standing in front of the ticket window and begging the booth worker to take his papers. Naturally, the booth worker, as well as the other passersby, was suspicious of this young man trying to pawn off these weird-looking documents. The man and I locked eyes, and he then asked if I was Jewish.

I responded, "Yes, I'm technically Jewish, but I'm not really Jewish."

The man looked at me, bewildered. My response only made him more desperate.

"Why do you ask?" I said.

The man replied that the papers he was holding were religious texts, which he wasn't permitted to carry past sundown. Having been raised Jewish and studied Judaism for many years, I understood what was going on.

The Jewish sabbath begins on Friday evening at sundown and doesn't end until the following evening. Once the sun touches down, you are not allowed to engage in any type of "work." This includes things like driving, using electricity, engaging in business, and apparently walking with certain types of religious documents. Whatever this man was carrying fell into the broad category of "work." To add another layer of complication, in the Jewish faith, all religious texts must be safeguarded with extreme care. This means that you cannot haphazardly dispose of them or leave them lying around. If these documents are ever to be discarded, they must be buried per Jewish law.

So, although this man couldn't simply abandon the papers he was carrying, he also wasn't permitted to walk with them past sunset. To complicate things even more, the man didn't want me to carry them either because I told him I was a Jew. In his mind, if he handed me the papers, he would be forcing me to sin as well.

"It's okay," I told him. "I would be happy to hold onto these until tomorrow night."

The man was reticent. He genuinely didn't want me to

bear the incredible onus of carrying these papers past sunset. I explained that while he may have viewed me as a martyr, I didn't care. At the end of the day, these were just pieces of paper with writing on them.

It soon became clear that I was his only option. After a minute or two of carefully deliberating his alternatives, the man finally acquiesced. I assured him that I would keep the papers safe until the following evening. All he had to do was call me, and I would meet him outside my building.

By this time, the sun had almost completely set, and the man was late for his evening prayers. Since it was now the sabbath, the man could no longer write my number down. Nor did he have a phone. I wasn't carrying a paper or pen, and the man was in a rush. He asked for my phone number and then repeated it to himself several times. I was doubtful that he would remember.

But, alas, the next night, right after sundown, I received a call from a random number. It was the man, and he was ready to come and pick up the papers. I was amazed. He must have spent the entire night repeating my number over and over again in his head. Shortly thereafter, I met him outside my building and gave him back his papers. He was far more appreciative than the situation warranted. I recognized that this man's life was so dominated by Judaism that I had essentially prevented him from committing what is tantamount to a crime, carrying serious repercussions.

What struck me the most about this encounter was how frantic this young man was. It wasn't just anxiety. This man was *scared*. He was terrified about the consequences he may face if he was unable to properly safeguard these religious documents. He was afraid of angering God. In this man's mind, God would not only be angry, but God would also punish him for these blasphemous acts.

I'm not sure what this man would have done if I had not offered to help. Maybe he would have tried to hide the papers somewhere or maybe he would have stayed at the subway stop until sundown the next day. Either way, I felt sorry for this man. I considered what life must be like with religion taking such totalitarian control of your existence. This man is so deeply entrenched in religion that his ability to function in normal society is greatly impaired. This is probably one of the reasons why the Hasidic community is so insular. They have no other choice.

Even in the less extreme, Orthodox Jewish communities, people's lives are highly regulated and guided by a set of arbitrary rules. For example, certain kinds of meat are okay, while others are prohibited. On the sabbath, not only is work prohibited, but they cannot even use electricity. But there are loopholes. For example, they are not allowed to turn on a light switch, but if a light is already on, or if someone who is not Jewish turns on a light for them, it is okay. Similarly, they are not allowed to push the button for an elevator, so they have special elevators that stop on every single floor continuously throughout the sabbath. This is obsessive-compulsive behavior in the most literal sense. It's borderline insanity.

These examples demonstrate how an obdurate approach to religion creates inherent contradictions. Some of these issues were not a problem thousands of years ago when Judaism was first founded. But as our society has progressed, instead of evolving, Judaism has simply tried to adapt. Are we really to believe that God has authorized the use of electricity, so long as you don't push a button or flip a switch yourself?

To its credit, Judaism has evolved in some ways. For example, animal sacrifices are no longer a regular part of the practice. Somewhere along the line, it was decided that God no longer required its continuation. So, why can't it evolve in other ways?

Regardless of what I say, I believe that everyone is entitled to pursue their spiritual paths. But I'm going to share my honest opinions and be critical of policies and practices that I think are far too antiquated for our twenty-first century society. This is particularly true for religion, which creates an "us versus them" mentality. It unifies certain subsets of the population while ostracizing others. This creates a lot of animosity through ignorance and misunderstandings.

But if religion is supposed to bring us closer to God, closer to consciousness, ourselves, and *others*, do we need all of these rules to do that?

This highlights what I believe is the most important distinction between religion and spirituality: where religion derives its authority from external sources, spirituality draws its power from being inwardly focused. Indeed, the emphasis on individuality is at the core of spiritual practice. In many ways, spirituality is the inverse of religion.

That said, we certainly don't have to abandon our religious beliefs to become more spiritual. Religion can enhance our connection to the Creator and galvanize our sense of oneness to all of humanity. As we will discuss in the next chapter, this is, in essence, what the Law of One asks us to do. So, rather than rejecting religion outright, we can instead seek a balance between our spiritual practices and our religious beliefs by avoiding any bright-line restrictions that would otherwise impede our spiritual progress.

CHAPTER 3

SHATTERING THE
RELIGIOUS PARADIGM

An Introduction to the Law of One

Many of us search for answers in religion, which, at its core, is the belief in a higher power. We put our blind faith in the idea that there is a God who has a plan for us. When good things happen, it's because God is rewarding us. When bad things happen, it's because God is angry or because God works in mysterious ways. Instead of looking for solutions introspectively, we diminish our accountability by empowering God with the power to determine all outcomes.

I find this way of thinking to be inadequate and antiquated. We are each born with certain inherent limitations. These limitations are only magnified by the challenges of life. We develop coping mechanisms. We pray that these challenges have a greater cosmic meaning. We conform ourselves to religious strictures that most of us were simply born into and never chose in the first place. We hope that the sacrifices we make will ultimately be rewarded in an afterlife. But perhaps we should approach life from a different angle, one where we embrace the unknown with the understanding that these very mysteries are what aid most in our spiritual evolution. After all, if life had no mysteries and we already knew everything there is to know, then we would have very few lessons to learn and very little purpose on this planet.

This is where the Law of One comes in. The Law of One is a series of tape-recorded question and answer sessions taken between Dr. Don Elkins, a physics professor, and a higher source of intelligence speaking through his friend, Carla Rueckert, while she was in a partially conscious, trance-like state.[2] The "source" of this material describes itself as a group of collective entities who, although once similar to us, has since merged into a single consciousness. This source has no apparent ego or agenda. Instead, it consistently reminds the listener (or reader) that it's simply a "messenger" and should never be idolized or venerated.[3] According to this source, this caution is particularly important because its past attempts to provide this information were distorted and ultimately evolved into what became many of today's major religions.

I understand that this is a fairly provocative statement. If true, it would completely change the bedrock upon which religion is founded. But if this source (or messenger) did have contact with different people and cultures throughout history, then it could certainly explain the similarities in the stories and belief systems that developed into the various mainstream religions. It's like the game of telephone: although the original message was identical, it became distorted over time as it was passed down from generation-to-generation. Perhaps this messenger even once had a physical presence on our planet. This could explain why the Bible refers to the presence of angelic beings called seraphim or cherubim. Even the term "angel" stems from the Greek word *aggelos*, which means "messenger." Perhaps these messengers appeared angelic to the people on this planet at this time.

So, although they might have explained that they were merely messengers, the people receiving the message may have been so awestruck that they couldn't help but to deify these seemingly godlike beings. This is similar to how our society treats celebrities. We know that celebrities are just normal people, but we seem compelled to venerate them anyway, as if they are greater than us in some way. It's a strange phenomenon. But it could very well explain why many people have difficulty believing that spirituality is an exercise in introspection rather than something that is derived from an external force.

The Law of One's communication is purely benevolent. The source is clear that its singular goal is to work "in service of the One Infinite Creator" by assisting humanity to become more aware of our true identity. In the very first Law of One session, the source opened the dialogue by stating that it had only one important statement: "all things, all of life, all of the creation is part of one original thought."[4] It's as simple as that. We're all just part of one singular thought. At its essence, this thought can be simply understood as consciousness. Beyond this concept, all other things are far less consequential.

The Law of One expands on this concept:

> Let us for a moment consider thought. What is it, my friends, to take thought? Took you then thought today? What thoughts did you think today? What thoughts were part of the original thought today? In how many of your thoughts did the creation abide? Was love contained? And was service freely given? You are not part of a material universe. You are part of a thought. You are dancing in a ballroom in which there is no material. You are dancing thoughts. You move your body, your mind, and your spirit in somewhat eccentric patterns for you have not completely grasped the concept that you are part of the original thought.

These few sentences alone are loaded with thought-provoking questions and information. Our very existence is shaped by our thoughts. Thoughts permeate our physiques and form the foundational structure of our belief systems. This passage challenges us to assess the literal construction of our thoughts and analyze whether we ever allow these thoughts to serve a greater metaphysical role in our lives. It challenges us to set aside the superficial thoughts that inundate our consciousness and contemplate the reason we are blessed with the ability to think at all. We are told, "you are not part of a material universe. You are part of a thought."

Think about this for a moment. If this is true, then what we perceive to be the physical (material) world is nothing more than an illusion predicated on thought. This passage seems to imply the inverse of Rene Descartes's famous statement "I think, therefore I am." That our existence is not proven by our ability to think, but rather our existence literally *is* thought. We are told that the emphasis of our thoughts is misplaced because we haven't yet come to terms with the fact that our existence as material beings is merely a façade. In reality, we are a collective of thoughts, a collective consciousness that is merely "part of the original thought," which perpetuates itself as all of creation. By this logic, our (perceived) existence in the physical realm has a greater significance and purpose. Otherwise, we would simply remain in a state of pure thought.

Before we can begin to understand our purpose, we must first recognize that we have a purpose. Maybe part of our purpose is to allow our souls to experience consciousness in a way that is impossible to do in a state of pure ethereal consciousness. Perhaps this is how our souls learn and evolve. According to the Law of One, the reason they're assisting us is that they're part of a larger group that's responsible for "guiding, protecting, steering, and managing our collective evolution on earth."[5]

So, if this source is authentic and truly wishes to help our planet, why do they not just appear and help us?

Well, according to the source, before they can reveal their presence on a planetary level, our species must first *acknowledge* their existence and then "invite" them to assist. Otherwise, they would be infringing on our collective free will by interfering with our natural course of spiritual evolution. In other words, the spiritual evolutionary process requires that humanity first recognize that we're a single entity or consciousness. Understanding this concept will open the door to a greater understanding of our connection with others both on this planet and throughout the infinite universe.

If you're still skeptical, that's okay. I understand. Even if you get past the idea that the source of the Law of One material is a higher form of intelligence, it might still be difficult to understand the motivations of such a group to assist our planet. But think about what our society would look like if our country progressed to a point where pain, suffering, dishonesty, and greed no longer exist. A place where everyone had their essential needs taken care of and where struggle no longer exists. I dare say that we would seek to help other nations. Now envision this happening on a global level. Think about what our world would look like after a hundred, a thousand, or even a million years. Where might our species turn our focus if we sought to help other civilizations enjoy the same benefits?

We Need to Break Through the Conditioning

This is one of the most important, albeit overlooked, spiritual resources ever created. The Law of One is both a philosophical principle and a title to a series of books containing information of a metaphysical nature. Even those of you who are already knowledgeable about spirituality are unfamiliar with this topic. This is probably because the information contained in the Law of One was obtained from an unconventional method: an allegedly intuitive source.[6]

I'm sure that some of you are incredulous. This reaction is understandable and entirely consistent with how we've all been conditioned to respond to seemingly unconventional ideas. Again, this is probably the reason why the Law of One has never received the attention it deserves. But, before you dismiss it entirely, let's assess our skepticism through a broader contextual lens. Let's consider why we might react so viscerally to ideas that don't conform perfectly to our traditional beliefs. For starters, we've been conditioned to be suspicious of anything that is seemingly obscure. Unfortunately, corruption has become so prevalent in our society that instead of fairly assessing new ideas, we often dismiss them immediately. It's purely visceral and likely nothing more than a defense mechanism we use to protect ourselves from being taken advantage of or from feeling embarrassed.

Think about the sidewalk preacher or the quintessential conspiracy theorist. We are exposed to so much hysteria daily—especially since the advent of social media—that we have trained ourselves to ignore anything even remotely abstract (no, I do not wish to be "saved" today, but thank you). Although this is an understandable and often necessary response, it has caused us to become overly cynical and intractable in our thinking. We cling to traditional paradigms to maintain stability. We become defensive over any ideas that threaten to alter the status quo. It's certainly easier to live in a world where the answers to all of our questions are gently spoon-fed to us and neatly arranged than a reality in which we must explore the depths of the unknown.

Let's put aside our past experiences, shelf our cynicism, and approach these seemingly abstract ideas with an open mind. Let's not let our fear of being judged by others affect our conclusions. After all, religion itself is based on some pretty outlandish stories and principles. Yet, religion has been so ingrained in our psyche that most of its eccentricities are easily overlooked. The reason that new spiritual ideas might invoke criticism is that they challenge our established paradigms and introduce ideas that at first blush might seem somewhat whacky. But most religions rely on ancient texts, most of which originate from sources that today would be labeled "unconventional."

For example, according to Judeo-Christian beliefs, Moses was a prophet who spoke directly to God. These concepts are so inoculated into our historical narratives that they are easier to digest than some of these new ideas. Ironically, if a religious leader today—or any person for that matter—proclaimed that they spoke to God, we would lock them in a padded room and probably refer to their followers as a cult. Yet, many of the same people who would be skeptical of a modern-day prophet are also the most ardent proponents of their religion and its ancient texts. Just because a concept may be new to you or outside of your immediate comfort zone does not diminish its validity.

Take a step back for a moment and try to imagine how it would sound if you tried to explain your religion to an extraterrestrial visitor from another planet. How would we answer this visitor's inevitable question of "Where's the proof?" How would we defend our religious beliefs from a position of logic or science? How would we defend our religion over someone else's?

It's quite likely that our responses to this visitor would be based mostly on faith. We intuitively believe in the existence of a higher power. We may not even be able to fully articulate the reasons for our belief. Either way, our explanation would probably fall short of a scientifically logical response. But this does not mean that what we're saying isn't true.

Imagine if Moses were alive today and that he's the president of the United States. One day, President Moses announces that he's going to hold an emergency press conference about an urgent matter of national security. Reporters all rush to the White House and huddle up in the pressroom. All of the reporters begin to speculate with their respective networks on live TV about what this urgent matter could be.

Cue the press conference. Moses approaches the podium and addresses the nation: "My fellow Americans. I have spoken directly to God and he has provided me with a list of commandments that each of you must follow…" How absurd would that sound? Certainly, an overwhelming majority of us would think the president had gone insane. We would call for his immediate resignation or begin impeachment proceedings (and rightfully so).

Very few people in today's society would be willing to believe that Moses spoke to God. Yet, most of our modern-day religious institutions are founded on similar—and often, even more outlandish—supernatural occurrences. As we saw in the previous chapter, some people even base their entire existence around these stories.

So, just as it's possible that Moses channeled a higher power to formulate the concepts contained in the Old Testament, it's equally possible that others throughout history, including today, have successfully connected with a higher form of intelligence. We're too quick to believe that these eponymous biblical figures spoke to a higher source of intelligence, but immediately dismiss the idea that someone in modern society could tap into a similar source. We should not blindly accept the validity of religion simply because it has been around for so long. If anything, this is why we should question it, especially if we're striving for progress and advancement.

I think it's important to keep an open mind rather than being overly cynical. Just because the information stems from an "unconventional" source doesn't make the information, or the conduit of this information, any less credible. Extreme cynicism and paranoia are certainly understandable in today's society, where deception is exposed on an almost daily basis. We're inundated with so much information in real time that it can be nearly impossible to curate fact from fiction.

I think our efforts to find purpose, meaning, and understanding in a world that can often be cruel and unforgiving has compelled us to personify this energetic force. We have labeled it God and used it as a way to explain the things that happen in our lives. We have ascribed human characteristics to this entity, which is infinite, limitless, and divine. This is an almost comical contradiction. Over time, this has created an endless variation of superstitious rituals and belief systems. We have become collectively manic and convinced ourselves that to keep this God happy, we must engage in these superstitious rituals and act according to a very particular set of rules. In turn, we hope that our conduct is adequate to please this God and prevent him from becoming angry and doing vindictive things, like flooding the world (again). We believe that this allows us to better control the narrative of our lives.

So, we conform to a set of predetermined rules. Each of these differs depending on our particular religious beliefs. As long as we follow these rules, God will spare our planet from another self-inflicted catastrophe or, at the very least, ensure a blissful afterlife for our souls. For the most extreme religious adherents, these are the driving forces that control the outcome of every decision they make. The salvation sought through this type of religious fanaticism is derived from external sources, instead of from within. This is a form of self-imprisonment. It has provided the opportunity for many unscrupulous people, and power structures, to manipulate and maintain control through fear.

We do not need religion to be spiritual. I think one of the problems with religion is that instead of uniting, it often creates division, even within its ranks. Next to politics, I can hardly think of a more polarizing topic. Yet, for some, it's probably comforting to believe that there's an omnipotent being who can answer their prayers—albeit discerningly—particularly in difficult situations.

I want to be clear that I'm certainly not diminishing the power of prayer as a general concept. I will discuss prayer and meditation in a later chapter. I think that our collective positive thoughts can heal and promote peace. The difference is that I believe the key to this great power lies not in the hands of an external entity, but within each of us. The more we focus our collective energies toward a common goal, the more powerful it becomes.

On the other end of the spectrum are people who don't believe in any god whatsoever. For these people, everything that happens in this world is the result of random chance and their conduct has no broader spiritual implications. These people are free from the traditional constraints of organized religion that would otherwise require their dedication and obedience to God. They believe in the "YOLO" (you only live once) concept and focus their energies solely on the physical world.

I think that very few people fall squarely into one side or the other. Perhaps the truth falls somewhere in the middle. On the one hand, maybe all of our actions do have some type of spiritual significance. But, on the other hand, maybe what happens in our lives has nothing to do with God punishing or rewarding our behavior.

The Law of One explains the complexity of our existence with the following analogy:

Let us give the example of the man who sees all the poker hands. He then knows the game. It is but child's play to gamble, for it is no risk. The other hands are known. The possibilities are known and the hand will be played correctly but with no interest.

In time/space…the hands of all are open to the eye. The thoughts, the feelings, the troubles, all these may be seen. There is no deception and no desire for deception. Thus much may be accomplished in harmony but the mind/body/spirit gains little polarity from this interaction.

Let us re-examine this metaphor and multiply it into the longest poker game you can imagine, a lifetime. The cards are love, dislike, limitation, unhappiness, pleasure, etc. They are dealt and re-dealt and re-dealt continuously. You may, during this incarnation begin—and we stress begin—to know your own cards. You may begin to find the love within you. You may begin to balance your pleasure, your limitations, etc. However, your only indication of other-selves' cards is to look into the eyes.

You cannot remember your hand, their hands, perhaps even the rules of this game. This game can only be won by those who lose their cards in the melting influence of love; can only be won by those who lay their pleasures, their limitations, their all upon the table face up and say inwardly: "All, all of you players, each other-self, whatever your hand, I love you." This is the game: to know, to accept, to forgive, to balance, and to open the self in love. This cannot be done without the forgetting, for it would carry no weight in the life of the mind/body/spirit beingness totality.[7]

This rather lengthy passage is jam-packed with incredible insight. So, let's break it all down and figure out what it means. In a broader context, this passage is essentially intended to explain not only why our souls choose to incarnate in the physical realm but also why these lifetimes must be challenging. After all, life would certainly be much simpler if we were born with an innate understanding of what our true purpose on this planet is. And the desire to understand our purpose is uniquely human. Indeed, a dog is simply a dog and cannot question the nature of its existence. It knows only how to be a dog and is motivated solely by its primal instincts. But when human beings incarnate, we must develop our own sense of identity. We don't really know who we are, who we may have been in a past life (although, as I will later explain in chapter 7, this isn't always the case), and what we're here to accomplish.

This passage attempts to explain why this is necessary and how it helps in our spiritual evolution. So, just as we would find no challenge in playing a game of poker where we already knew everyone's hands, our souls would gain very little from a life experience lacking in mystery or tribulation. We replay these experiences over and over again in myriad ways and, in so doing, hopefully gain even a perfunctory understanding of our capacity to experience and—perhaps more importantly—balance the wide gamut of emotions that facilitate our existence. Our ability to learn and grow from these experiences are the "cards" we each hold. The only way we can see someone else's "cards" is to "look into the eyes." Our eyes are truly a gateway to the soul, meaning that when we look into someone's eyes, it creates an empathetic response through which we recognize our shared humanity and thus our oneness to all things.

The sole purpose of the "game" we call life, according to this passage, is to open our hearts completely to *all others*, without exception, by embracing the love frequency. Recognizing our oneness with others empowers us to be more tolerant, more accepting, and "to know, to accept, to forgive, to balance, and to open the self in love." These are the lessons we must learn and it "cannot be done without the forgetting, for it would carry no weight in the life of the mind/body/spirit beingness totality."

This means that life cannot be assessed in a vacuum. We instead must take a holistic approach. This starts with the recognition that life has an infinite spectrum of possibilities. We should strive to see the underlying spiritual meaning in all outcomes and accept that our ability to fully understand the spiritual implications is limited by our finite senses. The religious archetype asks us to accept that these outcomes are the result of God's will. The spiritual archetype promotes the idea that these outcomes are the result of our design. The religious archetype is constrained by a well-defined set of rules and customs. The spiritual archetype is fluid. The religious archetype is obsessed with creating and enforcing rules to control and to create a semblance of structure and purpose. Spirituality is predicated on the idea that our souls are unbounded by any of the arbitrary and superstitious restrictions imposed by religion.

The inundation of rules imposed by the religious archetype can make us feel confined. It can be suffocating. It can cause resentment toward our religion and toward those who are not constrained by the same set of rules. This can manifest itself as rage, intolerance, rejection, and rebellion. This is not to say that religion doesn't serve a very important function in our society. It encourages good moral conduct and provides many with a sense of purpose and community. But it can also lead to oppression.

As I said earlier, having spiritual beliefs and believing in some type of "higher power" doesn't require that we spend our lives worshipping this force. Instead, I believe that it's enough to simply recognize that each of us comprises just a small part of a singular whole. We need not constrain ourselves with a set of arbitrary "rules" supposedly given to us by this unpredictable god-figure. I mean, what type of megalomaniac would put us on this Earth solely to worship and serve at his behest? I refuse to believe that our sole purpose on this planet is to serve God by following a set of archaic and oppressive rules. I refuse to accept this circular logic.

So, let's start with a simple concept: we are all connected to the same infinite source. There's no need to expand this concept any further. But we can use it to live a positive and compassionate lifestyle. Think about it like this: if we're all connected to the same source, then we are also connected. If we're all connected, then, at least at the core level, we all share a single consciousness. If we all share a single consciousness, then we would want to ensure that our conduct not only benefits us, but that it also benefits everyone around us.

This is the concept of acting in "service to others," which we will discuss more in the final chapter. This essentially means that we should treat others the same way we treat ourselves. In so doing, we are advancing both our own spiritual goals and the spiritual goals of humanity. This obviates the need to cling to an archaic system of rules to guide our lives.

That said, I certainly don't think it's unreasonable to have religious beliefs, generally. As I said earlier, religion serves a very important function in our society. I'm simply trying to extract the spiritual components at the core of religion and expand on these topics. It's counterproductive to confine ourselves within a prescribed set of religious constructs that precludes us from accepting new ideas.

Think about where we would be as a society if our attitude toward technology remained as obstinate as our attitude toward religion and spirituality. Technology never would have evolved, and our lives would be much less comfortable right now. Just as innovation is necessary for the advancement of technology, so too is innovation necessary for the advancement of spirituality. Thwarting progress is destructive and counterproductive.

So, the Law of One tells us that we are each part of a singular consciousness shared by all sentient beings throughout the universe and that our purpose here is to further explore this concept through our shared interactions with others. We will discuss the concept of a collective consciousness in more detail in the next chapter. I also encourage you to further explore this material for free by visiting LawofOne.info, as it contains a wealth of additional insights and information.

CHAPTER 4

DEVELOPING A COLLECTIVE
CONSCIOUSNESS

Religion, Science, and Spirituality

Throughout history, there has been an ongoing battle between religion and science. Despite the potential for harmony and balance, these two sides have been at odds. One refuses to recognize the legitimacy of the other. They have become mutually exclusive constructs. In many ways, this is similar to the political divide. Although many of us probably subscribe to a variety of beliefs from all sides of the spectrum, we tend to align ourselves with one specific political party. Of course, there are many practical reasons for this, but in reality, most of us are probably independents.

In the spiritual context, I've noticed that an increasing number of people are beginning to take a more "independent" spiritual approach. The past decade has seemed to galvanize some type of spiritual renaissance. More and more people are beginning to reject the traditional religions. The echo of this revolution is palpable. Every day, I see evidence that so many people feel spiritually abandoned. They are searching for an approach to spirituality that is less draconian than traditional religion and that better reflects our current values.

Until recently, religion has held a monopoly on spiritual ideas. Similar to politics, although we might each have differing views depending on the issue we're faced with, we're essentially forced to align ourselves with one of the predominant ideologies. This has effectively polarized our society into competing ideologies. Each ideology has its ardent proponents, who espouse their beliefs and are convinced that their perspective reigns supreme. They scoff at the idea of adopting new ideas that threaten to undermine their core beliefs.

This has led to visceral, erratic, and irrational responses to mere ideas, which alone pose no threat. Humanity has justified countless wars and atrocities in defense of the so-called truth. The battle seems endless, and no side will ever be able to fully claim victory.

Our evolution has reached a critical apex where religion and science must become less obdurate and learn to work together in harmony. The emergence of spirituality, like a third-party political candidate, offers the potential to gracefully blend these two competing ideologies.

Spirituality has no cookie-cutter molds. Science encourages innovation but is reticent to accept the spiritual implications underlying many of its conclusions. Religion is similarly rigid and resistant to any type of reform. It discourages constructive criticism or debate and rejects many scientific principles. Instead, religion often relies on fear to achieve subservience. But such mindless engagement in these traditions has resulted in religion becoming a lifeless shadow of its origin, creating generations of "zombie zealots."

For some people, these traditions are easy to follow. But I think a growing number of religion skeptics are beginning to question these practices. Many people are tired of religion's archaic views on social issues and humanity as a whole. This is particularly true amongst the younger generations, who appear to be more inquisitive and iconoclastic, myself included. I think that many of us find it difficult to accept any tradition that lacks a logically coherent basis. After all, why should we conform to a set of principles solely because an antiquated religion has demanded that we do so?

Religion has been corrupted and distorted to the point where its fundamental tenants, which would otherwise have the power to unite, are instead buried beneath a mass of politics, propaganda, and hysteria. The current state of our religious culture has created an "us versus them" mentality, causing us to be suspicious of other religions. We perceive ourselves as different from those who belong to other faiths.

We vehemently defend our religions and view those who disagree as our competition. The irony is that most people are defending a religion that they never had the opportunity to choose in the first place. They were simply born into it. We are indoctrinated to believe that the customs and traditions of our respective religions are the preeminent truth. We are taught that the other religions got it wrong. So, these religious debates are more visceral than logical.

The current religious archetype merely perpetuates this indoctrination rather than truly educates its followers on spirituality. This is incompatible with the unity and introspection central to spiritualism.

Religion insists that we look outside ourselves for God. Science looks to the natural world. Spirituality, however, encourages us to shift this focus within. Our souls are born free. We are inherently empowered with the tools necessary to create our belief systems. Yet, we imprison ourselves by conforming to a set of rules that we never agreed to in the first place. This is probably why the same people who identify with a particular religion tend to pick and choose what rules to follow. It's hard to follow all the rules. It's far easier to make distinctions based on what's convenient to us, even if these choices are anathema to religion.

I don't think that religion itself is the problem. I think the real problem is the fear-based control system through which religion is implemented. This is incredibly divisive and fails to deliver on its promise to deliver peace and harmony. So, instead of acting as a tool for spiritual enhancement, religion becomes more of a chore. We simply "go through the motions" instead of seeking any genuine spiritual introspection.

Consequently, the tenets of unity and love that are integral to religion have been perverted. We have all witnessed firsthand how the misguided religious views of a tiny segment of the population can lead to horrific atrocities and have a deleterious effect on society. No religion is exempt. This has made the current religious archetype antiquated and untenable.

This has caused many of us to reject traditional religion in search of a more holistic spiritual approach that incorporates our own life experiences, which have a direct impact on our ever-evolving spiritual outlook. But this search can leave us feeling isolated, abandoned, and bereft. We search for answers and meaning in a seemingly unforgiving and increasingly chaotic world. We want to believe that our existence has a greater purpose. But we are constantly inundated with fear of violence, death, poverty, and desolation. This can make us feel desperate and alone, even when we have solid support systems. We do our best to cope. We compromise. We settle. We try to find balance. We work jobs that are tolerable enough to survive. We live superficial lives that lack the real passion and meaning we are searching for. We strive to maintain the status quo. We accept artificial and self-imposed restraints. We medicate and self-medicate. I am not exempt.

Having a more spiritual perspective allows us to take a step back from the challenges we face and recognize that the physical world is merely an infinitesimal portion of our infinite metaphysical existence. This will lead to a heightened awareness of our true purpose on this planet. By developing a spiritual consciousness, we can vindicate the innate feelings of grandeur that many of us possess as children; the belief that we are destined for something greater than just the status quo but that tends to dissipate with age as we start to perceive this way of thinking as naïveté. By simply acknowledging that we are all interconnected and serve a unique and important purpose, we can change the way we approach both science and religion and make great strides in our collective evolution.

The Law of One's founding principle is that there are no absolute truths beyond the unity of our consciousness. According to the Law of One, "you are everything, every being, every emotion, every event, every situation. You are unity. You are infinity. You are love/light, light/love. You are. This is the Law of One."[8] In essence, we are all part of a singular consciousness. Take a moment to digest the magnitude of this statement.

This means that the separation we perceive is an illusion. In actuality, we are a singular entity and a unified identity. This is not a particularly novel concept. It was recognized by one of the most brilliant and influential scientific minds of the twentieth century, Albert Einstein:

> A human being is a part of the whole, called by us "Universe," a part limited in time and space. He experiences himself, his thoughts and feelings as something separated from the rest—a kind of optical delusion of his consciousness. The striving to free oneself from this delusion is the one issue of true religion. Not to nourish the delusion but to try to overcome it is the way to reach the attainable measure of peace of mind.

This statement is an excerpt taken from a letter written by Dr. Einstein in 1950 to the political director of the World Jewish Congress, Robert S. Marcus, expressing his condolences after Mr. Marcus's son passed away. It suggests that perhaps science and spirituality are not mutually exclusive concepts after all. Maybe these two concepts are wholly intertwined.

Dr. Einstein's statement certainly aligns with the collective consciousness theory, and supports the theory that our perception of separation is merely illusory and we are each but a fractional portion of a singular consciousness, which itself encapsulates the universe. Dr. Einstein states in no uncertain terms that it's mankind's failure to acknowledge this truth that imprisons us in our minds, inhibiting our spiritual growth. According to Dr. Einstein, the true purpose of religion is to help guide us toward this unity. Therefore, the solution to all of humanity's problems is to shatter the façade of separation and fully embrace that we are all one.

Dr. Einstein's statement demonstrates that many seemingly abstract metaphysical concepts are not so abstract at all. The problem is that many people have been conditioned to reject any idea that doesn't comport with mainstream thinking. As a result, many concepts are perceived as esoteric and ridiculed despite the abundance of scientific evidence. This is especially true for those ideas that threaten to destroy the religious paradigm and reshape the way we perceive our existence.

Religion has existed for so long that it has become ingrained in our society's ethos. Concepts such as the Law of One are foreign to most people and have therefore not received as much mainstream acceptance. Many of these seemingly new ideas have been labeled "new age." This has an unfortunate stigma perpetuated by critics who seek to diminish the credibility of these ideas and the people who espouse them. Ironically, these same critics who attack these so-called new age concepts for lacking "tangible" evidence are the ones who cling to religious beliefs that are themselves founded on mythology and rhetoric, rather than tangible proof.

I was initially drawn to The Law of One because it levels the playing field. There is no hierarchy. Everyone (and everything) is equal. Mainstream religion, on the other hand, is incredibly hierarchical and divisive. This impedes our spiritual growth.

The fact that religion is separated into different denominations and sects demonstrates the culture of inclusivity and discord perpetuated by religion. This is also evident in the process of religious conversions. If religion truly viewed everyone as equal, then a conversion process that requires people to overtly affirm the tenets of that particular faith would be unnecessary. Everyone would simply be accepted with open arms and no questions asked.

My idea of what spirituality should be excludes all pretense, judgments, and hard-line rules. I like to view it as a system of "collective individuality" by which we share a collective consciousness while also maintaining our autonomy. We experience unity and individuality simultaneously. Thus, we experience our individuality collectively.

The idea that human beings share a collective consciousness is nothing new, even in the realm of mainstream science.

The renowned twentieth-century psychiatrist Carl Jung discussed his theory on what he referred to as the "collective unconscious" more than half a century ago. According to Jung, the collective unconsciousness is comprised of elements of the human subconscious that are not the result of our personal experiences, but that is inherited and from a "collective psychic substratum."[9] Jung describes the elements of the collective unconscious as "archetypes," whereas the elements of the "personal unconscious are chiefly the feeling-toned complexes, as they are called; they constitute the personal and private side of psychic life."

Jung believed that human beings are connected through a collective unconscious that is comprised of "the whole spiritual heritage of mankind's evolution, born anew in the brain structure of every individual."[10] So, although Jung theorized that human beings share an innate and subconscious knowledge of our ancestral roots, he refused to hypothesize about the origin of this knowledge. Jung only superficially grazes the metaphysical significance of his theory.

Despite Jung's reluctance to address the metaphysical connection, the spiritual implications of his collective unconscious theory are vast:

> In this way there arises a consciousness which is no longer imprisoned in the petty, oversensitive, personal world of the ego, but participates freely in the wider world of objective interests. This widened consciousness is no longer that touchy, egotistical bundle of personal wishes, fears, hopes, and ambitions which always has to be compensated or corrected by unconscious counter-tendencies; instead, it is

a function of relationship to the world of objects, bringing the individual into absolute, binding, and indissoluble communion with the world at large.[11]

Here, Jung's theory echoes a theme expressed in Einstein's letter nearly ten years earlier. We imprison ourselves with the illusion that we are separate and isolated from the rest of humanity. This is what Jung describes as our "personal unconscious"—the part of our psyche that keeps us trapped in the fallacies of the material world and perpetuates our selfish and self-loathing tendencies. Jung appears to be saying that the "collective unconscious," on the other hand, is the part of our psyche that transcends the "petty, oversensitive, personal world of ego." The collective unconscious is the part of our physique that is inextricably intertwined with the "world at large," and allows us to observe the world objectively and to operate without the bias and egocentricity that otherwise dominates our behavior in the material world. Thus, when we activate our collective unconscious, we are operating in the "wider world of objective interest" rather than the venal world of subjective interest.

But Jung's analysis remains carefully scientific, avoiding any metaphysical innuendo. He compares the collective unconscious archetypes to inherited biopsychological and physiological traits. Jung avoids any literal suggestion that we share a unified consciousness. In so doing, the result is a sterilized and watered-down version of a collective consciousness that limits the spiritual experience entirely.

Lest there be any doubt, Jung went on to write an entire book admonishing his critics for their "often misunderstood" interpretations of the collective unconscious archetypes.[12] He argues that he never suggested these archetypes could ever be represented by a singular image or symbol, as "it would be absurd to assume that such variable representations [of these archetypes] could be inherited."

Jung provides clarity by explaining that it's not an archetypal image that remains constant, but rather the motif: the meaning underlying a particular image. For example, there are "many representations of the motif of the hostile brethren, but the motif itself remains the same." Yet, the archetypes of the collective unconsciousness "are without known origin: and they reproduce themselves in any time or in any part of the world— even where transmission by direct descent or 'cross-fertilization' through migration must be ruled out." Although this seems to imply a metaphysical connection, Jung explains that any such suggestion is purely incidental.

Of course, if Jung were to accept the inverse position, he would be forced to admit that at least part of his theory has a fundamentally divine element. But Jung, like many scientists, would rather classify the origin of the collective unconscious as "unknown" than accept any spiritual correlation. Perhaps Jung's reticence stems from the scrutiny he invariably would have received from his peers, likely diminishing the credibility of his work.

So, despite the clear scientific evidence linking metaphysics and science, many in the scientific community (especially the older generations) have been reluctant to explore these connections. Many skeptics are probably afraid that defending such a position would subject them to the same type of ridicule as Jung. Imputing spirituality into their scientific research could certainly compromise the integrity of their life's work. Others may simply be too stubborn to accept any concept that falls outside of the conventional scientific lexicon. This intractable approach is no different than a religious zealot who refuses to eschew archaic traditions to the detriment of progress.

Ironically, this type of obstinance is anathema to science, which encourages innovation and advancement. This is why Albert Einstein was such a renegade. He was not afraid to be outspoken about the relationship between science and spirituality. Dr. Einstein paved the way for later generations of scientists to consider this connection and to think outside of the proverbial box. So, whether Jung feared professional reprisal or was simply too stubborn to accept this potential correlation, he nevertheless refused to bridge the gap between the collective unconsciousness and a unified consciousness.

While Jung seemed content to end the analysis here, I am not. I refuse to accept that science and religion are mutually exclusive concepts.

Science isn't the only culprit. Religious institutions have also gone to great lengths to suppress scientific innovation.

The struggle between seventeenth-century Italian astronomer and physicist Galileo Galilei and the Catholic Church epitomizes this battle. The "dispute between the Church and Galileo has long stood as one of history's great emblems of conflict between reason and dogma, science and faith."[13] Galileo angered the Catholic Church after publishing his book *Dialogue Concerning the Two Chief World Systems*, which challenged the traditional Ptolemaic system (where the Earth is the center of the universe) in favor of the Copernican system (where the Earth moves around the sun). The Church had long supported the Ptolemaic system.

One year after its publication, Galileo was arrested and charged with heresy. The book was banned by the Church. At his trial, Galileo "defended himself by saying that scientific research and the Christian faith were not mutually exclusive, and that study of the natural world would promote understanding and interpretation of the scriptures." Nevertheless, after being threatened with torture, Galileo ultimately recanted his findings as "abjured, cursed, and detested" and spent his remaining years under house arrest.

Galileo understood that science could lead to a better understanding of religion. But the Church was so obstinate in its refusal to accept any ideas that challenged its traditional beliefs that it was willing to resort to coercion and violence to defend them. This is certainly not a very Christian thing to do, nor is it a characteristic unique to Catholicism. Religions have maligned scientists for centuries and vice versa.

This mutual animosity demonstrates how polarizing an extreme ideological perspective can be. It has a chilling effect on progress. Neither extreme is good for humanity.

It also demonstrates a problem inherent in religion: it's inflexible and refuses to progress even when there's compelling evidence to support new ideas and even when these new ideas have the potential to benefit mankind. The problem is that most religious institutions are hardly any more progressive today than they were centuries ago. For example, the Catholic Church didn't even admit that its persecution of Galileo was wrong until 1995, more than 350 years later. And that was only after a thirteen-year investigation!

My point is that if religion supported mistaken scientific principles 375 years ago, well before any of our modern scientific advances, it's certainly very likely that it still supports some very antiquated ideas today, too. No religion is exempt. On the flip side, if both Galileo and Einstein were willing to recognize the confluence between science and metaphysics, there's no reason why modern science can't do the same.

The Convergence of Science and Spirituality

The relevant inquiry is: where do religion and science converge? Better yet, perhaps the more relevant inquiry is: where do these concepts *not* converge?

Let's revisit what the Law of One says: all of creation, all life, all things are part of one original thought.[14] So, what is the building block of creation and thought? of consciousness?

Well, I think this question can best be answered by exploring the idea of energy. Now, I'm no scientist, but I'm certainly able to understand some very basic scientific principles. Scientists have already proven that the fundamental building block for all of existence is energy. According to the first law of thermodynamics, the total amount of energy in existence has always remained constant. Energy can neither be created nor destroyed.[15] This means that energy is infinite. What changes is not the energy itself, but rather the form that the energy assumes.

So, what are these different forms of energy?

Well, two of the most basic forms are potential energy and kinetic energy. An example of potential energy is the gravitational potential stored in a boulder being pushed up a hill. An example of kinetic energy is the energy of the boulder in motion as it begins rolling down the hill. The sum of these energies is referred to as "mechanical energy." For example, the heat stored inside of a hot object is the mechanical energy of the object's atoms and molecules in motion.

Even our bodies are made up of energy. Chemical energy is a form of potential energy that is stored in molecular chemical bonds within our bodies. This allows us to move. "Other forms of energy include electromagnetic energy, or light, and nuclear energy—the potential energy of the nuclear forces in atoms. There are many more. Even mass is a form of energy, as Albert Einstein's famous $E = mc^2$ showed."

This means that at its very core, energy and mass (matter) are interchangeable.[16] They are the same thing just in different forms. We may not perceive them this way, but nature surely does. So, under the proper conditions, mass can become energy and energy can become mass. Think about the practical implications of what I'm saying. This means that a beam of light, a brick, a telephone, and a peanut are all fundamentally the same thing. This is not me saying this. It's science.

Even the smallest portions of matter contain an extraordinary amount of energy. It wasn't until Dr. Einstein formulated the $E = mc^2$ equation that scientists were able to fully understand this concept.[17]

So, what does this equation even mean?

As a practical example, if we turned "every one of the atoms in a paper clip into pure energy—leaving no mass whatsoever—the paper clip would yield eighteen kilotons of TNT. That's roughly the size of the bomb that destroyed Hiroshima in 1945."

Holy cow, right? And that's just a paper clip! If we use the same equation to calculate the energetic equivalence of a 190-pound person, it will equate to approximately 1.86 million kilotons of TNT. To put this in perspective, this is about 88,403 more powerful than the 21-kiloton bomb that destroyed Nagasaki during World War II.[18] That is truly mind-boggling!

Okay, so you might be wondering how the heck any of this relates to spirituality. Well, according to science, energy is the building block of all matter. According to the Law of One, consciousness is the foundation of all creation.[19] By this logic, energy and consciousness are the same thing. They are synonymous principles. This means that energy *is* conscious. This also means that our existence is the product of this conscious energy.

But if we are all part of a single ubiquitous source of energy, then how can there also be so many individual pieces?

Well, we know that energy can neither be created nor destroyed. This means that consciousness can also neither be created nor destroyed. We also know that all matter (creation) stems from conscious energy. The fact energy can neither be created nor destroyed means that energy and consciousness have no discernable beginning or end. Consciousness is infinite.

Here is how the Dalai Lama tried to explain this concept during a discussion in London in April of 1988:

As far as logic is concerned, therefore, one would conclude that consciousness is beginningless because consciousness requires an earlier moment of consciousness as its cause, and that moment of consciousness would, in turn, require an earlier instant of consciousness. Therefore, it is infinite and beginningless. This kind of explanation may not be a hundred percent satisfactory, but, still, it has less contradictions and inconsistencies within it than any other.[20]

Here, the Dalai Lama brilliantly highlights the paradox of consciousness as it relates to the concept of creation. He extrapolates that consciousness is necessarily infinite because it cannot logically have a single point of origin that supersedes any other point of origin. Consciousness, therefore, must exist as an infinite perpetuation of itself. The Dalai Lama recognizes that although his explanation may not be completely edifying, it is the best explanation he can provide given our inherently and qualitatively limited capacity to comprehend that which is infinite.

Scientific Proof of a "Creator" and a Soul

If we accept that the scientific principles we just discussed are accurate, then our entire universe is built on energy or consciousness. Following this logic, because conscious energy has no discernable beginning or end, then at the most elemental level, all matter is identical. If this is true, then it's fair to conclude that consciousness is a singular entity from which all of creation is derived. This means that each of us is invariably connected on a metaphysical level by a collective consciousness. This supports the idea of what religion refers to as "God," or what I think is more aptly referred to as a "Creator." Building on this logic, although we are all built from and connected to the same conscious energy, we are each capable of perceiving ourselves to be separate from this source. This means that we each possess a portion of ourselves that is unique and as indestructible as the energy that created us. This supports the idea of a soul.

Before we go any further, I want to be very clear about something. When I use the term "Creator," it is nothing like the God that exists in most mainstream religions. We are taught that this God, although omnipotent, exists outside of us. Instead, when I use the term Creator, I am referring to a form of consciousness that is indivisible from ourselves. It is a conscious energy that, although mysterious and venerable, should not be worshipped or perceived as separate.

If consciousness is the building block of all matter, then our so-called physical reality is nothing more than an illusion. If we were to peel back all the layers like an onion, we would be left with only energy, with our collective consciousness. I would bet that the true and intended purpose of religion was to make us aware of this cosmic connection. But playing the game of telephone over thousands of years has left it distorted and confused. I think that this was precisely what Albert Einstein meant when he said that the "striving to free oneself from this delusion is the one issue of true religion."[21] Meaning, the purpose of religion is to break through the façade of physical reality and recognize our oneness with all things.

Science and the "Collective Consciousness"

The idea that we share a collective consciousness becomes even more apparent if we take our logic one step further to conclude that not only is all physical matter energy, but that thoughts are energy as well. This concept has gained increasing momentum in mainstream science, particularly in the field of quantum physics, where scientists like Albert Einstein study the nature and behavior of atomic and subatomic particles.[22]

The connection between energy and thoughts can be traced back to the 1800s and the double-slit experiment.[23] This experiment provided two fascinating insights. The first—and most intriguing—is that human observation directly affects the behavior of photons.[24] The second is that light can be both a particle and a wave. So, let's look at what this means and how it relates to spirituality.

In this experiment, scientists directed a beam of light toward a plate with two parallel vertical slits and a blank screen behind it. The expectation was that the light would shine through each vertical slit, creating two vertical slits on the screen.[25] Instead, the two light beams interfered with each other, forming a pattern of bright and dark bands on the screen. Even when a single photon was sent through alternating slots, one at a time, scientists still saw the same interference pattern, just as if the photon were traveling through both slits simultaneously.[26] So, even a single photon can produce the same interference pattern that is produced by a wave of light. "Basically, that means that all the *possible* paths of these particles can interfere with each other, even though only one of the possible paths actually happens."

But it gets even stranger. When scientists set up detectors to figure out which of the two slits a photon passed through, the interference pattern they had previously observed disappeared entirely.[27] This phenomenon occurred regardless of where the scientists placed the detectors. So, merely by observing a particle's path, even when the observation does not interfere with a particle's motion, the outcome will change.

More bizarrely, even when scientists delayed the measurement of a photon's path until after the photons had already passed through a slit—which should have provided the photon enough time to determine whether to take a single path or a superposition of two—there was still no interference. But it gets even weirder because it "doesn't work regardless of when that detection happens. Even if the second photon is detected after the first photon hits the screen, it still ruins the interference pattern. This means that observing a photon can change events that have *already happened*." This anomaly remains one of quantum physics' greatest mysteries.

To this day, scientists are baffled by this phenomenon. Why would human observation (thoughts) affect the motion of particles (energy)? Well, because thoughts *are* energy, too!

But the absence of a valid "scientific" explanation simply demonstrates the flaws inherent in such an obstinate scientific community. To accept this outcome would be to validate a metaphysical explanation. This would inevitably subject the proponent to ridicule in the scientific community. Yet, rejecting an idea simply because it doesn't conform to a conventional scientific archetype is the antithesis of science. This is precisely what the Catholic Church did to Galileo. But the shattering of an existing paradigm is exactly what a scientific breakthrough is!

Let's look at the results of this experiment. If I were presenting this argument to you, as a juror in a court of law, could I convince you that the results of this experiment prove by a preponderance of the evidence that our thoughts are evidence? Put another way, does the experiment prove that it is more likely than not that our thoughts are energy? As a trial attorney, I submit to you, ladies and gentlemen, that it does. After all, even the most brilliant scientific minds have failed to come up with any alternative theory!

As we have seen, the Law of One states that our existence is predicated on the idea that we are all part of a singular consciousness and that our material world is nothing more than an illusion. The scientific community has recognized that there is some hidden force that connects us through the collective unconscious but would rather ignore the metaphysical implications than accept the obvious relationship. Yet, the confluence between these two ideologies is obvious when we analyze the relationship between energy and consciousness—effectively synonymous terms. Following this analysis to its logical conclusion, we reach an almost unavoidable result: science has already proven the existence of an infinite Creator. Taking this one step further, because our thoughts are constructed of energy, and because energy is the building block of all matter, our thoughts can invariably create!

We will explore the topic of creation more in the next chapter.

CHAPTER 5

THE LAW OF ONE, CREATION AND BEYOND

How Did We Get Here?

As we just discussed, everything in the universe is the product of an infinite and unified conscious energy. Most of us are familiar with the story of creation that is told by religion: on the first day, God created light; on the second day, God created the sky and the sea…and so on. According to this story, despite the infinite number of stars and galaxies, mankind is at the center of all creation. We are God's pet project, a petri dish, alone in the universe.

Most of us are also familiar with the scientific explanation offered by the big bang theory, which states that the universe started as just a single point that stretched and inflated over billions of years to create the cosmos. No level of independent consciousness enters into the equation.

If you're anything like me, though, both of these theories have always fallen short. They almost seem a little lazy. Perhaps there's an alternative explanation that blends science and spirituality into a more satisfying narrative. According to the Law of One, the metaphysical world is mysterious by design:

> The one undifferentiated intelligent infinity, unpolarized, full and whole, is the macrocosm of the mystery-clad being. We are messengers of the Law of One. Unity, at this approximation of understanding, cannot be specified by any physics but only be activated or potentiated intelligent infinity due to the catalyst of free will. This may be difficult to accept. However, the understandings we have to share begin and end in mystery.[28]

That's certainly a lot to digest. First, it's important to understand what is meant by the term "intelligent infinity." This term is essentially synonymous with the term "energy." It's also what I've been referring to as "conscious energy." Intelligent infinity is the cornerstone of consciousness and all of creation. Intelligent infinity quite literally *is* the Creator. It is our collective consciousness. It is unity. It is all things.

The idea that the "undifferentiated intelligent infinity... is the macrocosm of the mystery-clad being" is similar to the explanation of consciousness we examined earlier from the Dalai Lama; namely, that the only way to reconcile the paradox of consciousness is to accept that it is infinite.[29] Similarly, intelligent infinity—which itself is the infinite consciousness/ creation—cannot be quantified, measured, or explained using a mathematical equation. While we are not asked to accept this explanation indiscriminately, we are told that these enigmas are part and parcel of the teachings. Just as the Dalai Lama recognizes that his explanation may not be entirely fulfilling, this passage suggests that this explanation "may be difficult to accept" as human tendency seeks a rational explanation even when a concept exists outside of what we may otherwise perceive to be logic and reason. Thus, our questions will inevitably lead to more questions.

For our exploration, however, I think it is enough to simply recognize that these paradoxes exist, rather than seeking to reconcile them using conventional methods. Indeed, our quest will be shrouded in mystery.

So, what does the Law of One say about creation?

Well, according to the Law of One, infinity is the first known thing in creation. Infinity *is* creation. It is the nucleus from which both consciousness and matter are derived. It is the unity that connects all things, and the unity that is all things. The unity itself is the only thing that truly exists.[30]

Just like energy, the Law of One explains that this unity is conscious. To better understand this concept, we can think of intelligent infinity as having two distinct parts: potential and kinetic. You probably remember from chapter 4 that potential energy is the energy stored in an object as a result of its position relative to some zero position, whereas kinetic energy is the energy of motion.[31] Here, the potential is "intelligent infinity" and the kinetic is called "intelligent energy."[32] Tapping into the potential (intelligent infinity) creates work. The work results in intelligent energy.

Admittedly, this can be a little confusing and perhaps even a little circular. But this is the struggle in trying to quantify and pick apart a concept that is by its very nature amorphous. The important thing to recognize is that intelligent infinity is conscious energy. Intelligent infinity is more akin to an understanding than it is to a concept that can be tangibly perceived. Words alone cannot adequately define an understanding.

Think about it like this: if I asked you to define the color green, what would you say? Certainly, you could describe the general properties of green. You could tell me that green is a color that sits on a spectrum between the colors blue and yellow. You could point to a blade of grass. But all of these descriptions presume that I have the gift of sight. If I were blind, these explanations would mean nothing. So, merely identifying the color green does not provide me with an understanding of what green is. Green's true essence cannot be articulated in words. The only way to truly understand the color green is to see it. I think this is similar to certain metaphysical concepts, like intelligent infinity.

As we discussed before, I think the concept of intelligent infinity discussed in the Law of One is identical to the concept of conscious energy that we discussed before. This is the scientifically supported principle that there is a single infinite source from which all of creation is derived and that we are all invariably connected on a metaphysical level. According to the Law of One, "the creation itself is a form of consciousness which is unified."[33]

Indeed, the Law of One states that "the first known thing in the creation is infinity" or energy.[34] Infinity then became aware (conscious).[35] The focus of this consciousness shifted into infinite energy or love.[36] This love-energy *is* the Creator. In this sense, the Creator can be likened to more of a concept than a deity that we should personify, like religion's concept of God. The Creator is essentially the process by which consciousness harnesses intelligent infinity (the potential), resulting in creation (the kinetic). This is the reason why I asked you to think of intelligent infinity as having two separate parts because it will help us better understand the process of creation.

I know that this explanation is way less sexy than the version given to us by religion. It's much more scientific and sterile. But the truth is, it doesn't matter. There is no real distinction between the Creator and the creation process itself because everything is one. In unity, there is an indistinguishable symbiosis amongst all things.[37] In unity, there is no polarity or disharmony, no right or wrong, but only identity.[38] This is exactly what the Law of One means: all things are, quite literally, one.

Two interesting points about the Law of One's explanation of creation are that first, it is predicated on the idea of consciousness, and second, it follows a very logical progression. The same cannot be said for either creationism or the big bang theory. Before we continue talking about the Law of One, I want to briefly discuss these other two theories.

Creationism is based on the idea that God already existed and that he created the universe in a week. Well, six days taking into account the one day of rest. I've always been amused by the idea that God, an all-powerful deity, would require a day of rest. Does God still take vacations? Is running the universe less tiresome than creating it? Was that single day of rest enough for all of eternity or does he take off one day a week? Creationism also assumes that God abides by our concept of time, which is purely manmade and based on the cycle of the sun (which wasn't even created until the fourth day). Needless to say, there are a lot of inconsistencies.

The big bang theory is closer to the Law of One in its explanation. The big bang theory hypothesizes that the universe began as an infinitesimally small, incredibly hot "something," a "singularity," so to speak.[39] Over time, it expanded and cooled until it created what we see today. Nobody knows what a singularity is, where it came from, or why it appeared. This is fair considering that the concept of infinity has no beginning and no real explanation, either.

The big bang theory certainly makes sense, and I think it complements the Law of One. Certainly, they are not mutually exclusive. The expansion and cooling explained by the big bang theory could very well be a product of intelligent energy. The only real distinction is that the Law of One has an additional element underlying its explanation: consciousness. This gives science a spiritual twist.

So, what else does the Law of One say about creation?

The Law of One explains how the emergence and evolution of consciousness, of awareness, ultimately enabled intelligent infinity to discern a new concept: "finity," or the recognition that oneness could diverge from unity and explore "many-ness."[40] Within this exploration, there are infinite possibilities, meaning there is no end to many-ness. The exploration can, therefore, continue infinitely in an eternal present, all while remaining part of the same original thought. This was all the result of intelligent infinity's desire to explore and understand itself by creating portions of itself that could act freely and without limitation. The concept of free will is integral to this explanation.

This seems pretty logical, right? Once intelligent infinity became aware, it developed an identity. Intelligent infinity recognized that by departing from unity, it could utilize creative expression to explore an infinite realm of identities and possibilities. We are all a product of this creative expression, of this quest for intelligent infinity to understand itself. We are all part of one infinite identity.

This Information Was Distorted

Earlier, I mentioned that the source of the Law of One material had given this information at different times to multiple civilizations all over the world. Unfortunately, as time passed, this information became distorted.[41] The distorted versions of this information became what we know as today's modern mainstream religions. This makes sense if we think about how dense this information can be. I can certainly understand why people would want to alter this information to make it more palatable and appealing to the masses.

The best way to do this is to add context by using stories and creating mythologies for people to bond over. Visualizing the concept of intelligent infinity is tough. It's much easier to conceptualize the idea of a personified entity called God. So, instead of describing creation by using the term intelligent infinity, it was said that God created all things. This is much easier to understand and follow.

I think it's unlikely that these mythologies were originally meant to be taken literally. Over time, these mythologies were altered by different cultures until they began to resemble the religions we see today. The information became more and more distorted as it was passed from person-to-person, generation-to-generation. I also think that those who sought power recognized the potential to exploit these ideas to control the masses, turning benevolent concepts into malevolent ones.

Earth Is Not Alone in the Creation

I discussed how science has proven that all matter is energy, that all energy is conscious, and that all consciousness is unified. This is further explained by the Law of One and supports the idea that we are all the product of a single source of conscious energy. We can think of this conscious energy as the "Creator."

According to the Law of One, the fundamental building block of all physical matter is light (or limitless light).[42] Light is an intelligent energy. Light is the outpouring of randomized creative force.[43] Light is the first manifestation of intelligent energy that's visible to the naked eye.[44] So, when we observe light, we are getting a glimpse into creation and of the Creator itself. This makes light an incredibly powerful tool. The Law of One provides a very complex explanation for how intelligent infinity uses light to create matter. I've provided an oversimplified summary to move things along, but I strongly suggest reading the cited portions if you want a more in-depth analysis.

The "creative principle" is the process of creation through the exercise of free will.[45] The creative principle results in an "infinite reaction," where creative forces grow and expand, ad infinitum, creating energetic patterns.[46] These energetic patterns eventually become more intelligent and structured, creating physical matter.[47] These patterns form in holographic style, meaning that an infinite number of dimensions, universes, galaxies, and solar systems exist as one entire creation.[48]

One of the things I find most fascinating about the Law of One's explanation is that it implies we are living in a holographic universe. This information was provided nearly ten years before any of the holographic universe theories emerged in the 1990s. The holographic universe theory says that the information we perceive to be 3D reality is stored on a 2D surface, including time.[49] One way of simplifying this is to imagine a 3D film. Although a 3D film is not a hologram, it creates the illusion of 3D objects on a flat, 2D surface. But in our 3D universe, we're able to touch objects and we perceive that the "projection" is real. One of the major implications of this theory is that our perception of space and time is entirely distorted, meaning that space (and possibly even time) travel might be far less daunting than we had otherwise believed.

Another fascinating aspect of the Law of One's explanation is that our universe contains an infinite number of galaxies, solar systems, and planets. This means there is infinite potential that we are not alone in the universe. According to the Law of One, there are millions of planets in the Milky Way galaxy alone that have sentient, hominid beings![50] This statistic is supported by NASA's Kepler telescope, which suggests that about 20 percent of all stars host planets in a "life-friendly, habitable zone."[51]

Yes, I went there. As if this book weren't already weird enough, I dived into a subject that might be even more esoteric than spirituality: aliens! Not only are we not alone in the universe, but our galaxy is teeming with intelligent life. But, as you can see, this topic ties in perfectly with spirituality.

Let's take a step back for a moment and contemplate the nature of infinity. Consider the vastness of what it means to live in an infinite, perpetually expanding, and boundless universe. A universe in which we are merely an infinitesimally microscopic part. A universe that stretches on and on…and on.

Now, let's contemplate the opposite: that the universe is finite. At some inconceivably far distance, the universe simply ceases to exist and all that remains is a state of nothingness (whatever that may be). Even if this were the case, there would still be at least a hundred billion stars in the Milky Way galaxy alone. One hundred billion! This is an astonishing number. And this is in just our galaxy! Scientists estimate that the universe consists of at least one hundred billion galaxies. The number of stars this encompasses is practically incalculable and truly boggles the mind: about twenty billion trillion in the observable universe alone. For each star, there are individual star systems. For each star system, there are individual solar systems. For each solar system, there are individual planets.

With this in mind, let's now consider the argument that we are (and have always been) alone in the universe. That no other life has ever existed anywhere, even in the most remote and uncharted recesses of what we consider to be outer space. That we have somehow been the only planet to have ever seeded intelligent life, anywhere in the infinite depths of space and time.

Taking into account what we've already discussed, does this not seem a little absurd?

Let's put aside all of the so-called conspiracy theories. Let's table all the talks about flying saucers and alien invasions. Instead, let's use our logic and common sense. This can be more difficult than it sounds, not because we are illogical people, but because Hollywood has hijacked this topic. This makes any earnest conversation about extraterrestrials instantly taboo, or at the very least likened to fantasy or fanaticism. It becomes the type of thing that exists only in movies. Anyone who believes otherwise is viewed as either crazy or naïve.

Just because there are movies about aliens doesn't eliminate the possibility that aliens exist. Sure, it's entertainment, but perhaps some of these Hollywood writers believe there is truth behind it. Maybe Hollywood even mixes some fact with fiction. Who knows?

According to a 2016 study published in the scientific journal *Astrobiology*, it's "astonishingly likely" that we're not the only advanced civilization to have evolved in the universe. Even if we were to assume that the universe is finite and that intelligent life exists (or has existed) on only one in a trillion habitable planets (which is a conservative estimate), this would mean that there are (or have been) about 10 billion other intelligent civilizations.

I think it's a little egocentric to believe that no other life-form, not even a microbe, has developed anywhere else in the universe. Some believe that even if other intelligent civilizations do exist, the distance between our star systems and theirs is too vast for contact to arise. But this theory is based on the assumption that our perception of space and time is accurate. Remember, if there is any truth to the holographic universe theory, then space travel might be much less difficult than we had otherwise imagined. It wasn't too long ago that physicists believed airplanes were too heavy for commercial air travel to be possible, too.

What if there were a civilization with technology thousands, millions, or even billions of years more advanced than our own?

So, even mainstream science acknowledges that it's absurd to deny that other advanced civilizations either exist or have existed. I honestly believe that in the not-too-distant future, we will look back and wonder how the heck we were so naïve.

Our planet is no different than other civilizations throughout history who believed they, too, were alone. For example, until

1921, the Dani tribes of Papua New Guinea had no contact with anyone outside of their civilization. Due to geographical and technological constraints, the Dani were confined to a remote and difficult-to-access part of the world. This kept the Dani in and outsiders out. They had no idea that any other people existed on this planet. That is until the Dutchman Captain Van Overeem stumbled upon them in 1921.

To us, it probably seems obvious that a tribe of people could exist on the outskirts of a remote and mountainous region of our planet. We understand how large our planet is and we recognize the potential for undiscovered life. But, for the indigenous people who lived in these remote regions, the possibility of outsiders never arose. So, a civilization like the Dani couldn't even conceive of the types of technology that existed outside of their insular society.

Of course, as technology progressed, the Dani would have inevitably seen some type of aircraft flying overhead. This would have sparked curiosity and encouraged exploration. Simply by observing an airplane or helicopter (or drone), the Dani would have realized that they either share the planet with an advanced civilization or that an advanced civilization was visiting the planet.

So, let's bring this conversation back full circle. Perhaps our current civilization is the global analog to the Dani tribes. Maybe our geographical and technological constraints prevent us from truly comprehending the vastness of the cosmos. Maybe we can't fully appreciate the complexities of extraterrestrial technologies because they are beyond even our wildest imaginations. Perhaps our own comparatively primitive existence prevents our ability to grasp the abundance of life throughout the universe.

The Truth Is Out There!

From a spiritual perspective, the idea that we are not alone in the universe and that there are likely many civilizations that are vastly more advanced than us is critically important. It instills a sense of humility and forces human beings to recognize that we are not masters of the universe. Suddenly, our petty differences would become less important and we would quickly discover our collective humanity.

I have always recognized the connection between spirituality, metaphysics, and the unexplained. As a kid, I loved books about aliens and UFOs, and I was obsessed with the show *The X-Files*. One of the reasons I loved this show so much is because I've always felt like there was a tinge of truth to it, and I've always believed that the truth is out there. Just look at all the unexplained aerial craft sightings throughout history.

Let's take a recent example. In 2004, an eighteen-year-career U.S. Navy pilot, Commander David Fravor, was in the middle of a training exercise with his team of pilots when they were tasked with intercepting multiple unidentified flying objects in the area.[52] Navy officials had been tracking several dozens of these objects for weeks.

By Commander Fravor's own account, when he and his team arrived at the reported location, they observed an object that looked like a white Tic Tac. The object was about forty feet long and looked similar to one of the navy's Hornet fighter planes, except that it had no wings and was somehow just hovering above the water. The object created no rotor wash (the visible air turbulence given off by helicopter blades) and mirrored the pilots' movements as they pursued it. Then, it suddenly vanished without a trace. The object moved faster than anything he had ever seen in his life.

Very shortly after, a different team of pilots intercepted the object and were able to capture a video. In 2017, thirteen years after the event, the Pentagon finally released the video. This is also the year the Pentagon officially acknowledged the existence of a secret government program dedicated to studying unidentified flying objects (a.k.a. "UFOs") known as the Advanced Aviation Threat Identification Program.

According to *The Washington Post*, the existence and release of this video "marks one of the most significant disclosures about government research into flying objects."

A still frame picture taken directly from the video recording is shown below:

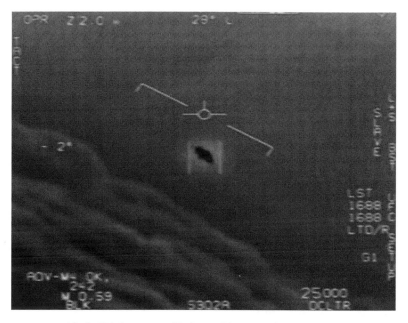

(*Credit: U.S. Department of Defense via* The New York Times/Redux).

Commander Fravor retired from the navy in 2006 but spoke very little of this incident until he was contacted by a government official investigating the event the same year. To this day, the nature and origin of the object remain a mystery. But Commander Fravor remains adamant about two things: the object was real, and it was "something not from Earth."

Keep in mind that Commander Fravor was no slouch. He retired from the navy as a high-ranking and well-respected officer with the rank of Commander. At the time of the incident, he was a veteran pilot with tens of thousands of hours of flight experience. He was also the commanding officer of the VFA-41

Black Aces, an elite U.S. Navy strike fighter squadron of F/A-18 Hornet fighter planes.

But Commander Fravor was frustrated by the whole experience. By his account, he didn't do drugs, he wasn't drunk, he got a restful sleep the night before, and it was a clear day. "I think someone should have looked into it," he said. "Having talked to some of the other folks, it's a big frustration that it's coming out now and wasn't discussed back in 2004." These are not the words from some UFO fanatic. Commander Fravor is a decorated military pilot and an expert in his field.

Of course, the craft could have been the product of one of our government's top-secret projects. This is certainly possible, but unlikely considering that our navy pilots were tasked with intercepting it. Even if it was one of our government's aircrafts, it begs the question: how did *we* develop this incredibly advanced technology in the first place? It's also unlikely that the craft would belong to another country, considering that the U.S. military budget in 2017 was $610 billion, with the next closest country being China, with a military budget of just $228 billion in 2017.

I think the answer is clear: it's the craft of an advanced civilization. Surely, there are still many skeptics out there who will try to find an alternative explanation, even when no logical explanation exists. There are still many people who are so desperate to avoid believing in the existence of extraterrestrial life that they will resort to great lengths to remain in denial. But many other people have also come forward with information related to this topic. For example, in 2001, Dr. Steven Greer, a former traumatologist and founder of the Center for the Study of Extraterrestrial Intelligence held a press conference at the National Press Club in Washington, D.C., which included twenty retired military, government, and intelligent officials. Each of these people independently confirmed knowledge of, and experience with, extraterrestrial species. This is in addition to the dozens of other government officials, including NASA astronaut Gordon Cooper, all of whom corroborated this information. I know Dr. Greer personally and was fortunate enough to work with him on a small project. So, I can say with absolute certainty that he is genuine.

What's more, since I originally completed the first draft of this book, I felt compelled to come back and add a few recent and pertinent developments in the area of UFO disclosure. The first is that in the summer of 2020, the U.S. government acknowledged the existence of a once-covert specialized unit dedicated to investigating UFOs, which has taken the place of another UFO-seeking Pentagon unit that was allegedly disbanded in 2012.[53] According to Deputy Secretary of Defense David L. Norquist, the purpose of the task force, now named the Unidentified Aerial Phenomena Task Force (UAPTF), is to "improve its understanding of, and gain insight into, the nature and origins of UAPs...The mission of the task force is to detect, analyze, and catalog UAPs that could potentially pose a threat to U.S. national security."[54] Then, in February 2021, documents released by the Pentagon through a Freedom of Information Act request openly acknowledge that the government has recovered and tested wreckage from numerous UFO crashes. The documents also reveal that the technologies recovered are far superior to anything that currently exists on Earth including a mysterious "memory" metal that can reassume its original form after being bent or crushed, and materials that can make things invisible.[55]

While this is a far cry from the full disclosure of the government's arsenal of intelligence in this area and is undoubtedly only the tip of the iceberg, it's certainly a step in the right direction and proves that—at least ostensibly— not only are there unidentified crafts in our airspace that the government simply cannot explain, but that our government has also recovered unexplainable technologies from the wreckage of these crafts. This is a huge revelation! No longer can the public deny the existence of UFOs or try to explain away sightings with illogical pseudoscience. And although I'm truly disappointed that the military would propagate the fear-based narrative that Hollywood has perpetuated about a potential alien "threat," it is not surprising and almost certainly for the goal of serving their agenda.

But instead of succumbing to fear, perhaps we can focus on the more positive aspects of the government's tacit admission and open our minds to the possibility that our planet could very well be a far more interesting place than we have been led to believe. To do this, we must each free ourselves from the decades of social conditioning that have instilled fear, cynicism, and paranoia into our physiques. We have to open our minds to the possibility that the individuals who control this information have lied to and deceived us to profit and maintain control. Again, I won't go too far down the rabbit hole in this book, but I do believe the hole runs deep.

Another major development occurred in December 2020 when the former head of the Israeli Defense Ministry's Space Division and highly esteemed professor, Haim Eshed, came forward with information that could change the future of humanity as we know it. In an interview with the preeminent Israeli publication *Yediot Aharonot*, Mr. Eshed—who had spent 30 years as the head of Israel's space program and is a three-time recipient of the Israel Security Award—stated in no uncertain terms that both Israel and the United States have been dealing with extraterrestrial civilizations for many years but have kept these relationships a secret because "humanity isn't ready."[56]

In fact, Mr. Eshed claims there is a "Galactic Federation" of extraterrestrials that have made agreements with the U.S. government in order to research and understand "the fabric of the universe."[57] A freaking Galactic Federation! Even more amazingly, Mr. Eshed claims that there is a secret underground base on Mars that has American and extraterrestrial representatives.[58] Mr. Eshed "insists that Trump is aware of them, and that he was 'on the verge' of disclosing their existence. However, the Galactic Federation reportedly stopped him from doing so, saying they wished to prevent mass hysteria since they felt humanity needed to 'evolve and reach a stage where we will…understand what space and spaceships are.'"[59] Given the public's pathological incredulity and tendency to panic, these concerns would certainly make sense.

Like Commander Fravor, Mr. Eshed is another highly accomplished, well-respected, and credible source with little to gain from coming forward with this information and explains that "if I had come up with what I'm saying today five years ago, I would have been hospitalized…today, they're already talking differently. I have nothing to lose. I've received my degrees and awards; I am respected in universities abroad, where the trend is also changing."[60] Certainly, the implications of what he's claiming are revolutionary (to say the least) and, if true, would reshape the existing social, political, and religious paradigms.

As crazy and far-fetched as much of this might seem, it is interesting to note that all of these recent disclosures coincide so closely with the creation of the Space Force as the fifth branch of the United States Armed Forces. Is this merely a coincidence or are we being prepared for the unveiling of something far greater than we could ever imagine? Only time will tell. But if we are to believe what Mr. Eshed claims (and, frankly, we have no good reason not to), then it seems that at least a certain compartmentalized subset of our government is already in contact with highly advanced civilizations who have apparently shared technologies that surpass anything we could ever have imagined. This would also mean that there are many highly advanced civilizations that have banded together to form what appears to be a benevolent alliance. Given that it is a *Galactic* Federation, one can reasonably deduce that the number of extraterrestrial member-civilizations is utterly massive. This would also mean that we already have the technological ability to transform into a highly advanced interstellar society and further suggests that a clandestine subset of the military-industrial complex perhaps already has. Once again, I will save this rabbit hole for another book. For now, at the very least, it provides some captivating food for thought.

Whatever you choose to believe, Mr. Eshed's revelations certainly provide a far more benevolent explanation for the presence of extraterrestrials and their intentions with our planet; namely, to further understand the nature of our universe. Perhaps these civilizations have evolved beyond the point of conquest and greed, to focus their quest inwardly on knowledge and understanding. It appears, however, that these entities are afraid that if they make their presence known to humanity we will react irrationally, as we often do. As a society, we are simply too spiritually immature. So, it unfortunately seems that until we reach a certain point of spiritual evolution, one in which we become a more tolerant and openminded, and less fear-based society, these beings will not reveal their existence. If nothing else, this alone provides perhaps a most compelling reason to seek further spiritual growth!

Let's Analyze This through a Spiritual Lens

How about, instead of acting scared or defensive, we view this topic through a spiritual lens. What are the spiritual implications that coincide with the existence of other advanced life-forms? Well, for starters, our planet would suddenly become much less significant. All of our superficial differences would become meaningless. The religious paradigms would instantly and permanently shift. Life, as we know it, would never be the same.

So, I think an essential part of spiritual progression is the recognition that we are not alone in the universe. Until mankind can learn to live harmoniously amongst ourselves, we cannot expect to have a peaceful relationship with other species. If I were a visitor to this planet, I'd be reluctant to divulge my existence until our society could learn to live in peace. We are far too impulsive and unpredictable. We are highly distrustful of outsiders and suspicious of their motives. Many of us would find it hard to believe that another species would visit our planet for peaceful or charitable purposes.

But where does this cynicism stem from?

A lot of things, probably. But certainly, a large part of the cynicism reflects our subconscious. We impute our values and mores onto others. This causes distrust. We can so easily convince ourselves that the only purpose for an ET visit would be conquest. As if a civilization that is light-years more technologically advanced than ours would ever need to exploit our planet's resources to survive.

I think that some of our incredulity stems from our reliance on a fiat currency system to survive. Most of us must work jobs to survive. We worry about food and shelter. If we are lucky enough, we also worry about comfort. Think about the progress our species could achieve if survival and comfort were no longer a concern. Think about what you would do if all of your basic needs were provided and you never had to work. The potential for happiness and prosperity would be limitless.

What would you do to occupy your time? What passions would you pursue?

We would probably be a more introspective society. We would turn our focus inward toward improving ourselves, both spiritually and physically. We would certainly get along much better. Eventually, we would probably begin to work together toward a common goal. We would seek to explore beyond ourselves, beyond our planet, into the greater cosmos. Maybe we would even reach the point where we felt it was our duty, or obligation, to help struggling civilizations and pursue a mutually beneficial spiritual quest. This would be especially true if we recognized that we are all part of the same consciousness shared throughout the universe.

I think another part of our skepticism is much more straightforward. Some of us simply have a difficult time accepting the idea that alien civilizations could exist. These types of skeptics demand irrefutable evidence (whatever that may be). As I mentioned earlier, I think Hollywood is a big part of the problem, having hijacked and perverted the idea of extraterrestrial life. Aliens are often depicted as terrifying creatures with malevolent intentions. This instills fear and makes us wary about their possible intentions. Very few movies portray extraterrestrials as beings that look and sound like us. They usually have a weird or scary appearance. Except for a few movies (e.g., *Contact* and the 2016 version of *Arrival*), most Hollywood films do not depict aliens in a positive light.

These movies also make us view the existence of extraterrestrials as fiction. It's something that only exists in the movies, as fantasy. The topic espouses images of people wearing tinfoil hats waiting for contact in the New Mexico desert. We ridicule those, like Commander Fravor, who have witnessed UFOs. We haphazardly explain away unusual phenomena using reasoning that make no sense. An inexplicable display of lights over a large metropolitan city witnessed and recorded by thousands of people is explained away as something like a weather phenomenon. This happened in Mexico City in 1991.

Instead of simply shrugging off these occurrences, maybe we should open our minds to other possibilities. Maybe that incredible display of lights in the sky is just an advanced civilization's way of saying hello, of introducing itself. Perhaps this is how an intelligent and cautious extraterrestrial society would acclimate our volatile species to the idea of their existence, rather than simply showing up at our doorstep, which would likely result in us greeting them with pitchforks. Think about how you would approach an animal in the wild. If you got too close, the animal would either run or attack. Most wild animals would not let you approach and pet it.

So, maybe the real question isn't why haven't they made contact, it's why haven't we noticed?

Another interesting point explained by the Law of One is that it would infringe on our society's collective free will and interfere with the natural course of our spiritual evolution if an ET civilization simply revealed its presence.[61] Before ETs can reveal themselves to us, we must first acknowledge their existence and then invite them to do so. A critical mass must open its eyes and recognize the existence of ETs before they can reveal themselves. An infringement on our free will would have karmic consequences. I think it's likely that any technologically advanced civilization would also be advanced enough spiritually to recognize this. Perhaps they even abide by a set of cosmic principles that we're currently incapable of understanding. Who knows, maybe even the source of the Law of One material itself is one of the forces behind some of the demonstrations of light in our skies.

We Just Need to Open Our Eyes!

Contact from a higher intelligence can come in many forms. Let's take, for example, the idea of crop circles. A crop circle is an area of standing crops that have been leveled in the form of a circle or more elaborate pattern. At first glance, one might try to explain away such phenomena. Certainly, some crop circles are the result of hoaxes. But others are truly inexplicable.

Let's take the Sri Yantra mandala crop circle formation. In 1991, a very large, perfectly formed, ancient Hindu mandala symbol called Sri Yantra was discovered etched into an isolated dry lake bed by Air National Guard pilots flying a routine training mission in Oregon.[62] The symbol measured over a quarter-mile in length. It was comprised of 13.3 miles of lines carved into very hard, compact dirt in a desolate area that prohibits vehicles of any kind. The lines and dimensions were perfect.[63] Each line was etched with laser-like precision, measuring exactly ten inches wide by three inches deep. There were no footprints, no tire tracks, no tool markings, and no signs that any of the dirt was removed. What's more, nobody else, pilots or otherwise, reported seeing this symbol before the date of its discovery. It simply just appeared.

Here are two pictures taken from different angles:

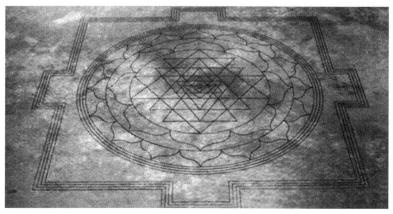

Source: Pepper Cox, "Sri Yantra Mystery: An Interview with Bill Witherspoon," *The Iowa Source*. 7, May 2019. https://www.iowasource.com/2019/05/07/sri-yantra-mystery-an-interview-with-bill-witherspoon/.

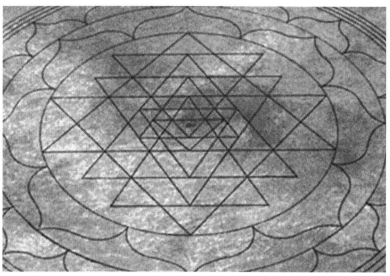

Source: "The Research Continues," *Sri Yantra: The Oregon Desert Mystery*. Accessed 16, Mar 2021. http://www.oregondesertmystery.com/research.html.

Just look at the incredible precision! It is flawless. If this was a hoax, it would have taken an incredible amount of time, skill, effort, and resources to accomplish, not to mention tools and technology that simply don't exist.

So, what exactly is the Sri Yantra and what is its spiritual significance?

The Sri Yantra is an ancient symbol.[64] It's a type of mandala with geometric patterns. A mandala is a plan, chart, or geometric pattern that represents the metaphysical cosmos of the universe. The Sri Yantra is formed by nine triangles that surround and radiate from the central point. These nine triangles are of various sizes and intersect with one another. In the middle is the power point, called "Bindu," visualizing the highest, the invisible, elusive center from which the entire figure and the cosmos expand. The triangles are enclosed by two rows of lotus petals, representing creation and vital energy. The broken lines of the outer frame represent a sanctuary with four openings to the regions of the universe.

The Sri Yantra is a very powerful symbol because it's built with "sacred geometry." This sacred geometry is a precise mathematical formula called the Golden Proportion of Phi ratio, which is considered to be the "blueprint of all creation." It's also found in many famous works of art including Leonardo da Vinci's *Vitruvian Man*.[65]

The Sri Yantra is considered to be the "mother of all Yantras," because all other yantras stem from it. Its name means "instrument for wealth." It can help solve all of one's problems and clear all negativity from one's life. A Sri Yantra can help one achieve a higher level of consciousness and create one's reality. This symbol is said to be a divine storehouse of energy that picks up cosmic waves emitted by the planets and other universal objects. It transforms these waves into positive vibrations, which are then transmitted to the surroundings where the Sri Yantra is placed, cleaning all energies of negativity.[66]

So, the question is: what's the significance of the Sri Yantra crop circle?

I think that there are multiple answers to this question.

The first answer is somewhat superficial. The higher intelligence that left this message is simply saying, "We exist. Open your eyes."

The second answer is a little more complex. I think the symbol itself provides several spiritual messages. One message is based on the fact that sacred geometry was used to construct the design of the symbol. The precision and symmetry embedded within the symbol remind us to recognize the unity of all things— to recognize our collective consciousness, our oneness.

Another message is based on the meaning of the Sri Yantra itself. Remember, this yantra represents material and spiritual abundance through the manifestation of our reality and the conquering of our limitations. This will lead to a higher level of consciousness and eliminate negativity, resulting in internal peace and harmony. So, the higher intelligence that left this symbol was reminding us that eternal prosperity is not only attainable but that it begins from within ourselves. Perhaps the symbol was even intended to galvanize the masses and challenge us to start the process so that we can begin to heal ourselves and our planet.

The last message is based on how this message was delivered. It appeared suddenly, as if by magic. This is certainly an intricate and extravagant way to communicate, by any standard. The symbol also appeared in the only form of communication that is quite literally universal: mathematics. This, again, reminds us to recognize our oneness with all things. The physical depiction of the symbol itself is a metaphor for our society's extraordinary potential to achieve a level of peace and prosperity that exceeds our wildest imaginations, once we recognize this one fundamental truth.

In this chapter, we discussed the idea that our existence is predicated on the principle that there is a *conscious* energy at the foundation of our collective consciousness and all of creation. This energy—or *intelligent* infinity—is at its essence a consciousness of pure love. In a desire to explore and better understand itself, this infinite consciousness (the Creator) separated portions of itself from the oneness using the frequency of love, all while remaining inexorably connected to a singular consciousness that exists outside of time and space in an eternal present. This creation stretches throughout an infinite universe that is teeming with a diverse range of intelligent life. And it appears that at least some of these intelligent life-forms have been sending us benevolent messages in the form of intricately woven sacred geometry depicting our cosmic roots. We just need to open our eyes. It's like the Beatles said: "there's nothing you can know that isn't known. Nothing you can see that isn't shown. There's nowhere you can be that isn't where you're meant to be. It's easy. *All you need is love.*"

CHAPTER 6

THE QUEST FOR SPIRITUAL TRUTH

Finding Our Target Audience

It is said that beauty is in the eye of the beholder. Then so must be one's spiritual truth. After all, what is beauty if not a form of truth? One's personal truth, like art and wine, is merely a matter of perception. Of course, there are certainly some universal truths, like the world is round and pizza is delicious (yes, that's a universal truth, too). But much of what we label as "truth" is quite subjective.

I had a very interesting conversation when I bumped into an old college friend recently, whom we will call Greg. We hadn't seen each other in about seven years. Greg is an aspiring comedian who's already achieved a moderate level of success and notoriety. He even made it to the final round of *Last Comic Standing*, a talent-based competition on NBC, and has earned several comedy segments on late-night talk shows. For nearly a decade, Greg has been honing his skills and working toward comedic success. He performs regularly at some of Manhattan's most iconic comedy clubs and recently went on tour with other comics to perform for American troops in the Middle East.

One of the first things I noticed about Greg was that he seemed happy. He may not yet have achieved the level of fame and fortune he desires (although I believe he will), but he is passionately following his dreams. Greg is living his truth. You see, Greg has never envisioned himself as a nine-to-five, "put on a suit and work" type of guy. That's not for him. No, Greg loves making other people laugh. He thrives on it. So, to Greg, comedy is not just an art or a passion, comedy is his spirit. It is his life.

Despite the cold, Greg and I stood on a street corner discussing our pursuit of happiness and success. I told Greg about this book. I wasn't finished writing it and I was having some creative setbacks. I told him about my writing process and my initial ambivalence to write it. We spoke about dedication and perseverance. We talked about the people who support us, and, even more so, those who don't. We agreed that there will always be people who don't understand our work, our message.

"But that's okay," Greg said. "Those people are just not your target audience."

"Great point," I said.

The truth is that none of us can make everyone happy, even if that's our goal. My writing, his comedy, anything subjective, will not appeal to everyone.

Greg and I also spoke about fears that sometimes inhibit our progress. The fears of rejection, failure, and being held accountable. We discussed how our critics can sometimes play into this fear. We discussed how some people resort to criticism as a defense mechanism because they themselves are unhappy. Some people view their success in direct relation to the success of others. Some people are too afraid to deviate from the status quo. Conformity can be much easier than living one's truth.

Greg mentioned that he will occasionally run into someone else from college who will say something like, "I was funnier than you," as if this somehow diminishes Greg's success and the quality of his work, or somehow elevates that person's status.

Each of us is on our individual path. We each decide what we feel is best for ourselves. But Greg and I both agreed that this does not mean we should allow the negativity of others to permeate our work. It's just as important that we use the negativity as a source of inspiration as we do the positivity. These encounters are all integral to the creative process, just as striking up a conversation with an absolute stranger can provide surprising inspiration.

What I admire the most about Greg, and what has truly inspired me, is that he trudges forward, no matter what. Greg believes that he is funny because Greg *is* funny. Greg knows that he's funny. If he wasn't, then he wouldn't make people laugh. He wouldn't keep getting work. But he does.

Sometimes Greg finds himself focused on the one person in the crowd who isn't laughing. This is just human nature, though, isn't it? We know that we can't appeal to everyone… but that doesn't stop us from trying. The way Greg handles these types of situations is to remind himself that if everyone in the audience is laughing except this one person, then maybe it's not Greg who's the problem. In this scenario, it's much more likely that the person laughing just isn't his target audience.

In the same vein, we cannot allow fear of rejection to interfere with our efforts to live our truth and find success. Rejection can often pave the road to our target audience. Each of us has one. We just need to discover where to look.

Finding a Middle Ground

Many works of fiction often depict human beings as skeptical and stubborn. Mystery and suspense films often feature a protagonist who has made a unique discovery, only to find that when he or she attempts to reveal what they have discovered, nobody believes them. For example, a child who just saw a ghost but whose parents refuse to believe them. We as the audience *know* that what the child experienced is real. We saw it for ourselves on the screen. We get frustrated when the child's parents simply dismiss the occurrence as a fantasy or lie. We are objective observers. This makes us privy to facts that the film's skeptical characters don't have access to. It makes us wonder how the characters can be so blind and naïve. Certainly, if we were in their position—if it were our child—we would handle it differently. We would believe our child. Surely, the film's characters are just too jaded to see the truth.

Often, the story's protagonist becomes obsessed with proving their beliefs with an incredulous cast of characters. The protagonist rarely waivers and works with all their might to discover the one piece of critical evidence that will vindicate their efforts and prove all of the skeptics wrong. This obsession usually coincides with what others believe to be psychotic behavior. Family members, friends, and sometimes even the audience begin to think the protagonist has gone mad. Sometimes, the protagonist even begins to doubt their sanity. Their insecurities worsen. Surely, everyone else can't be wrong. Eventually, the protagonist reaches the climax and finds a key piece of evidence, the missing link that ties everything together. They are finally vindicated!

Outside of fiction, we all have many opportunities to play both the protagonist and the skeptic. At times, we find ourselves fiercely defending or advocating for our point of view. Other times, we question the actions or beliefs of others. These dueling roles are critical to our evolution. When we defend our beliefs, it can strengthen our convictions and introduce others to new ideas. It also runs the risk of discouraging productive dialogue, which is harmful to our spiritual growth. Similarly, when we criticize others for their beliefs, it means that we are not embracing the empathy that is fundamental to spiritual practice. That said, our beliefs depend on our perspective and our perspective defines our ideologies. The problem becomes when we feel the need to become defensive (or offensive) without first allowing ourselves to assess a situation and consider both sides. We stubbornly refuse to realign our perspective and end up becoming that same skeptical parent who refused to believe that their child saw a ghost.

We all like to believe that we can remain impartial or at least open to new ideas. When we're passionate about our own beliefs, it can be difficult to see the other side. We often forget that there even is another side. It's only when we can accept that everyone is entitled to their own opinion, regardless of how crazy it sounds, that our discussions and debates can be productive. This way, instead of simply arguing, we can engage in intelligent discourse with the ability to compromise.

In the context of a debate, either side rarely offers the absolute truth, and there's usually a middle ground. This is why we call our individual beliefs "opinions." An opinion is simply a belief or judgment based on grounds that are insufficient to produce complete certainty.[67] Many of us often forget this and defend our opinions as if they're absolute facts. This is antithetical to progress. It's only through compromise that we can find real solutions.

The only real absolute truth is our own identity. Knowing who we truly are will give us the confidence to embrace new ideas and to further our connection with others. This brings us closer to a unified consciousness. Identifying our truth allows us to connect with our spiritual identity.

The question now becomes, how do we live our truth?

Finding Our Truth and Overcoming Insecurity

What does it mean to live your "truth"? Is this simply another new age cliché, like the phrase "it is what it is"? Or is there a deeper, more substantive meaning? This is, after all, a critical question in our spiritual quest. As I just mentioned, identifying our truth connects us to our spiritual identity, but the more challenging task is putting this identity to use.

Because we live in a world where a massive amount of information is readily available almost instantaneously, it can be difficult to discern between fact and fiction. I sometimes feel like there's so much information that there's no information. For every "fact," there seems to be an opposing and equally plausible "counter-fact."

So, how do we know what to believe and where should we get our information? I honestly have no idea. What I do know is that the truth inside us is something that we can always be certain of. So, let's explore this concept of inner truth, of our quest to find and live our truth.

What does it mean to live our truth?

It means different things for each of us and depends on our perspectives. At its core, living our truth requires that we honestly assess what is truly important to us and pursue opportunities that align with these things. This is often easier said than done. We face many external pressures to conform to a certain archetype. We often feel compelled to justify our actions (and even our thoughts) to others. We anticipate the reactions of others and tailor our conduct accordingly. Maybe we even constrain ourselves from doing something we want to do because we are afraid of how it will be received by others. We allow our egos to distort the truth. This, in turn, affects our decision-making process. We might say and do things we don't truly believe in just so we can fit in.

I have overcome many of my insecurities by distancing myself from these types of thoughts. I have recognized that a lot of my self-doubt and loathing stems from my fear of rejection. Deep down, I want to be liked by everyone and make everyone happy. I know that this is impossible, but it still creeps into my behavior patterns. For example, instead of giving my true opinion, I sometimes give an overly diplomatic response to avoid any possible confrontation. To avoid doing this, I have to remain mindful of these tendencies while putting aside my fear of rejection. I have also come to recognize that many of my so-called flaws are not necessarily faults. Of course, there are things about myself that I'm constantly trying to improve upon, like being more vocal about my true opinions, being more patient, and listening better. But being imperfect is simply being human. Instead of being insecure about our imperfections, we should embrace them. After all, nobody is perfect.

I'm still a work in progress. I've simply learned to better manage my insecurities by developing a system for coping with them. My process first involves identifying the root source of a particular insecurity. This requires lots of introspection and honesty. Next, I separate the problems I think are real from those that are merely superficial and predicated on ego. The superficial problems are the ones that negatively affect my life and thwart my spiritual growth. I disarm my insecurities by embracing them as a motivational improvement tool. So rather than letting my insecurities debilitate me, I use them as a weapon to combat the negative voice inside my head. Embracing my imperfections allows me to recognize that they are largely ego-driven and have very little basis in reality.

This has allowed me to work on the parts of myself that I needed to change, like things that affect my relationships with others and inhibit my spiritual growth. For example, one of the things I recognized about myself that I wanted to change was that I used to be very reactive in response to disagreements. My responses were based more on emotion than logic. I was easily agitated. I never made a genuine attempt to consider the other person's perspective. Instead, I imputed my belief system into a debate, under the presumption that my perspective was the only one that could be correct. But this was rarely the case. There is always room for compromise.

To counteract this behavior, I have taught myself to think before I react. This requires me to stop and analyze the situation. First, I assess my thoughts and emotions and then I assess the other person's. I try to understand where my reaction stems from: maybe it's a place of love, maybe it's a place of fear or judgment, maybe it's something else entirely. Regardless, when I force myself to stop and think instead of just reacting, I usually respond with much more empathy and compassion. This doesn't take much time, just a matter of seconds. But the result is usually far better than when I react without thinking. It often turns an unnecessary argument into a civil conversation. Remember, when we connect with others, we bring ourselves closer to cosmic unity.

Of course, this doesn't always work. If my counterpart is reactive or unreasonable, then it could quickly escalate the situation. Sometimes this can't be avoided. But in these situations, I find that the best approach is to be calm and remain patient. This usually makes it more difficult for the other person to remain angry and will help de-escalate the situation. I try to remain mindful of context and pick my battles wisely. For example, if I'm having a political conversation and the other person starts to get a little upset, I don't reciprocate the anger. Instead, I recognize that our opinions might differ on certain issues and simply digress. The odds that I'm going to change the other person's mind by escalating the intensity of the debate are slim. This will probably make my counterpart dig their feet in deeper. Sometimes, it's better to just agree to disagree and walk away.

This is not to say that I will never stand up for what I believe in. If somebody asks me for my honest opinion or agrees to a civil debate, I'm happy to oblige. There are also instances when I feel it's necessary to engage in a situation that I know could escalate in intensity. For example, if I believe that someone is lying or trying to take advantage of me or someone I care about, I will confront them. Or if I think someone is being a bully or acting in an unreasonable manner that could harm someone else, I will also intervene. But these instances are few and far between. More often than not, I look for a way to compromise.

When it comes to battling our insecurities, we are often our worst enemies. I sometimes catch myself in the act of self-sabotage, where I am thinking or acting in a way that reinforces my doubts. I know that this will sound obvious, but one of my greatest weapons against this is to exude confidence. Even in situations where I feel overwhelmed or outmatched, I act confidently. One of the greatest lessons I learned about being a lawyer is that half of the battle is just sounding confident in what I say. There are so many ambiguities in the law that I often find myself arguing for a position that isn't necessarily supported by the law, but that appeals to common sense. I may not always win, but I'm always amazed at how often my arguments are given credibility despite the lack of legal support.

I have applied this same "fake it 'til you make it" attitude toward every aspect of my life and it's resulted in nothing but positive things. The more I succeed, the more confident I become. This success provides a framework and reference point for future success.

This approach has also taught me to listen and follow my instincts. Being confident allows me to overpower the fear that would otherwise suppress my intuition. It's opened my eyes to the great success that all of us are capable of if we simply remain focused and dedicated to our goals. Being confident has also forced me to reassess what failure is. I think for most people, the concept of failure is failing to achieve an ideal or expected outcome. But I would rather fail to achieve the desired result 100 percent of the time than to have never tried at all. Failing to attempt is the only true failure because there are so many valuable lessons to be learned through adversity. I once had a boss tell me that there's no such thing as an "A for effort," there's only winning. I disagree. The effort is what has taught me how to become successful. I have learned exponentially more through my failures (for lack of a better term) than I have from my successes. Indeed, failure not only enhances my desire to succeed, but it demands humility and—consequently—greater compassion for and connection to all of humanity. Thus, failure brings us all closer to oneness.

Success is the ultimate goal, but we should not be afraid to try something simply because we're afraid to fail. The only time we truly fail is when we allow ourselves to be content with mediocrity due to an unjustified belief that we're not worthy of success. It's important to remember that success isn't only measured in wealth; it's also measured in our achievements, our impact on society, and our overall happiness.

Being Honest with Ourselves Is the Key to Revealing Our Spiritual Truth

As I said before, I'm far from perfect. But being imperfect doesn't prevent me from being spiritual. The key to spirituality is recognizing that we're all imperfect and bound to make mistakes. The challenge is to not only recognize this in ourselves and learn from our mistakes, but also allow others to do the same.

To live our truths, we need to recognize that even though we're all connected, our spirits are infinitely diverse. By embracing the differences in others without judgment, we are each encouraged to be the most genuine version of ourselves.

Of course, in the abstract, these are just words. But if you take a moment to reflect on these ideas, I think you'll agree that they make sense. Whether it's a career choice, a relationship, or an everyday decision, it's important to choose the path that best reflects our identity. This is how we feed our spiritual growth.

Choosing this path is not always easy. It's even harder when we're unhappy. We have all experienced unhappiness at some point in our lives. Think back to a time when you were unhappy. Consider why you were unhappy and how you escaped the situation. In retrospect, the solution seems obvious. But when you feel trapped, it is not always so easy. I sometimes reflect on the past and wonder why I had ever put myself in a situation that I know or should have known would make me unhappy. But hindsight is twenty-twenty. As I will soon explain, it's not always so clear while we're living in the moment.

I don't think we can avoid adversity simply by living our truth. Adversity is a necessary part of life. Adversity is how we learn. It's how we grow. Living our truth liberates us from the shackles of conformity. It provides us with opportunities for happiness because we're following our genuine interests rather than the superficial nonsense society tells us we need.

This is easier said than done. It's not like we can just up and quit our jobs tomorrow to pursue our passions. But what we can do is take small steps, like picking up a hobby that allows us to explore our creativity. It doesn't matter how we do it. The important thing is to find something that makes us happy and we pursue it. This might mean we have to make sacrifices in other parts of our lives. Maybe this means staying up an hour later or getting up an hour earlier. Whatever it is, I think you'll agree that the sacrifice was worth it. Remember, our souls evolve the most through sacrifice and discomfort.

Two things that help keep me grounded are working out and writing. I usually fit in both of these things very early in the morning. The exercise keeps me stable, focused, and healthy, while the writing keeps the creative juices flowing and makes me feel more fulfilled. I am a deeply spiritual person and feel most fulfilled when I'm helping others. Writing provides a way for me to blend these things in a productive and rewarding manner.

My Struggles

This is a good time to share a little more background on who I am. On a metaphysical level, it's a cathartic process to share these feelings in this forum. I hope that this will encourage each of you to be more open about your struggles so that you can work toward overcoming the suppressed negative emotions that impede your spiritual growth.

I was married for almost three years. In retrospect, I *knew* it wasn't going to work. I went through with it anyway. The bottom line is that I ignored my truth.

Let's assess it from a spiritual perspective.

Even while I was living through my marriage, I knew that I wasn't being honest with myself. I knew that it was toxic to me, my partner, my family, and my friends. I could feel the negativity thwarting my spiritual and creative progress. This was an incredibly isolating feeling. I felt like a caged animal because I couldn't be myself. I suppressed my true self. This led to fights. The fights led to more fights, and it ultimately ended in a divorce. If you were to ask my family or friends about that period of my life, they would each express the same sentiments: I was a shell of my former self.

We weren't right for each other. Now that the marriage is over, the true Randy is back. I have absolutely no regrets. It was a learning experience and it's all part of the journey. My marriage, just like every other experience in my life, led me to this very moment. The literal moment we decided to divorce, not only did I feel liberated, but I also felt a surge of inspiration come pouring in. I started writing almost instantaneously, and these words would form the basis of this very book.

So, although the marriage was traumatic, it forced me to put my life in perspective and assess what was necessary for me to live my truth. This would not have been possible without this experience. I learned the value of true partnership, compromise, and patience. Above all, I learned that the most important thing is being honest with myself. This is the only way for me to attain true happiness.

This learning experience has also taught me to be cautious as I move forward. I try to avoid making the same mistakes by analyzing important decisions with my "honesty filter." This means stripping away the superficial layers and deciding whether a particular decision is right at a fundamental level. For example, I'll ask myself whether the decision I'm choosing is truly for myself or if it's what I think people expect of me. As much as I love helping others and believe that it's part of my journey, I can't genuinely do so unless I'm happy with my path. It's not selfish to seek happiness. It's only selfish to seek happiness at the expense of others.

The Outrage Culture

So, what is the truth and who gets to decide?

I think truth is in the eye of the beholder. It's all about perspective. One person's truth might be another person's antipathy. There is an infinite number of variables that affect what we believe and how we feel about certain issues. From a metaphysical level, when forming our opinions about certain issues, it's important to remember that if we do have a shared consciousness then we should try to approach every situation with empathy. This doesn't mean we have to acquiesce or agree on issues we don't believe in. What it means is that we shouldn't try to impose our beliefs onto others. It's okay to have a respectful debate, but we should do so with the understanding that what we believe to be true isn't necessarily true to someone else. With a few rare exceptions, just because someone takes the opposite side of an issue doesn't mean that person is wrong; it just means they have a different perspective. Truth is in the eye of the beholder.

Having empathy allows for more genuine human interactions and serves the greater good. Kindness serves the greater good. Generosity serves the greater good. Actions serve the greater good. But words and opinions alone do nothing to serve the greater good. Without empathy and compassion, words pose a much greater risk of polarizing and angering. But for grown adults, words alone shouldn't have the ability to incite such rage. Words don't cause any tangible harm. It's the meanings that we associate with words that create the blueprint for how we react. Our minds give salient meaning to words, which create visceral reactions that rely on several different factors like who said it, the intonation, the context, and our preconceived biases.

This is why freedom of thought and expression is so important. Truth is often quite subjective, even though we sometimes act like things are black and white. But all of us should feel free to express our thoughts without fear of reprisal. My personal beliefs should have no bearing on the ability of someone else to express their beliefs and vice versa. Free speech is integral to a free society. Unfortunately, I think many of us have lost sight of that.

Freedom of speech should be exactly that: *free*. It doesn't mean free unless I disagree with your opinion. There are some exceptions to this rule such as speech that is intended to incite violence. But what I'm talking about here is purely opinion-based speech. This type of speech should never be censored. A person is entitled to have whatever belief they want, irrespective of whether it comports with our own beliefs or value system.

I'm sure most of you are familiar with the famous adage adapted from Voltaire: "I wholly disapprove of what you say but will defend to the death your right to say it." I think the significance of this saying cannot be overstated. Even if I disagree with another person's opinion, I wholeheartedly respect their right to say it. If someone says something I do not agree with, I simply express my own opinion and move on. I don't take it personally. I don't fight. And I most certainly don't become hysterical.

Someone will inevitably say something that we believe is stupid or offensive. Instead of taking offense, perhaps the better approach is to take a step back and assess that person's intentions. Maybe they're genuinely ignorant or misinformed. Maybe they're insecure. Maybe they have a different set of experiences and worldview. Or maybe it was just a really bad joke. Whatever the case, we all need to be more tolerant of others' opinions. I think that once we truly start viewing everyone else as equal—once we understand our metaphysical connection—we can transcend these superficial divides. If we all worked toward this same unifying goal, then we can make significant strides in eliminating these misunderstandings entirely. This will force us to recognize that our so-called differences are meaningless. So, let's trade our judgment for understanding, our anger for empathy, and our resentment for compassion. This will create a far more balanced and harmonious society. By unifying to this degree, we would be making further strides toward recognizing our oneness.

I understand why people are offended by certain topics. I recognize the inequities of the past and wholeheartedly support our efforts to remedy them. But I think there's also a point where our tendency to label and divide has an adverse and polarizing effect. On a spiritual level, I think these divisions take us further away from our sense of oneness. This is the type of stuff that keeps me up at night.

I recently woke up in the middle of the night thinking about how divided we have become. I thought about all the needless hate and oppression. How superficial and ridiculous it all is. How simple the solution is if we could just agree to treat each other equally based on what's inside rather than how we look on the outside. If we could all agree to set aside our egos, our pettiness, greed, and perceived differences and simply recognize our shared humanity.

We each need to recognize that we all sometimes say and do silly things. Sometimes completely by accident. Rarely, if ever, does a comment alone call for the level of hysteria that seems to be the default position taken by so many of us right now. The constant witch hunts need to stop. Nobody is perfect. We have all said and done things we've regretted. Not everything is always so black and white. We need to lighten up. We need to provide an open forum for creativity, self-expression, and humor. We need to allow ourselves to poke fun at uncomfortable topics. This provides a certain therapeutic catharsis as it forces us to recognize the existence of unpleasantries without getting lost in the minutiae. Are there certain lines that should never be crossed? Certainly. Genuine bigotry, for example, is something most of us would agree is always unacceptable; however, just because a "line has been crossed" doesn't mean the person who crossed the line had any malicious intent. Sometimes we have to separate the actor from the act. A bad joke or genuine ignorance are two examples of how a line could be crossed without any malice. When this happens, instead of attacking the speaker or becoming enraged, let's instead have a civil conversation about why we are upset. If it was an honest mistake, then a simple apology should be sufficient contrition. Lesson learned. On the other hand, if the person intended the comment to be hurtful, we could express our disapproval and move on. A heated debate will simply serve no purpose.

We need to stop being so uptight. We need to stop with the witch hunts. We need to end this "outrage culture" we're living in. Nobody wants to walk on eggshells all the time.

There will always be inherently polarizing topics— like religion, gender, and race (to name a few). So, it's almost impossible to discuss any of these issues without saying *something* that offends at least *someone*. This has absolutely nothing to do with politics, although we seem to make everything political these days. This is about the freedom of our minds, bodies, and souls. But our society seems obsessed with analyzing every word we say under a vernacular microscope and then categorizing the speaker into a particular group based upon their thoughts (or at least their thoughts in the moment). We're so incredibly reactive. We're impulsive. We make immediate assumptions. We allow very little room for error and give second chances only to those whom we selectively determine "deserve" a second chance. So many of us have embraced a culture of recreational outrage where mass hysteria is not only the new normal, but it's also what's expected.

I think part of the problem is that we see injustice all around us, both domestically and abroad. But we don't know how to react, and we don't know whom to truly blame. Our anger remains suppressed. It festers. It lies in wait until it finds a suitable outlet. We search for culprits. We seek targets. We blame politicians. We blame the rich. We blame the police. But "suitable" doesn't necessarily mean appropriate. So, we latch onto causes that, at least ostensibly, offer a solution. We choose sides. We conform because it feels safe. We immerse ourselves in groupthink. We become afraid to offer an opinion that deviates from the party line.

The problem with this mode of thinking is that it inhibits progress. It creates an "us versus them" mentality. It needlessly polarizes issues that could otherwise be resolved through reasonable discourse and compromise. We go on the offensive and act impulsively. We ignore and attack opinions that don't conform to our beliefs. Instead of unifying, we create labels that ostracize those who refuse to acquiesce to the status quo. Unity becomes conformity. We all allow ourselves to get so caught up in our causes—in our idea of justice—that we become illogical. Our arguments become more visceral than substantive. It becomes form over substance. We act like we support free speech but get angry when someone's opinion offends our sensibilities.

While the following two examples are somewhat dated, I still think they are relevant and typical to our conversation.

The first example is from June 2nd, 2017, when Bill Maher, the host of a popular television program on HBO called *Real Time with Bill Maher*, and who is white, dropped an offensive racial slur. Now, those who know and watch Maher know that he's not a racist. He was just trying to be funny, but he undoubtedly crossed the line.

Here's an excerpt from a *National Public Radio* article summarizing the encounter:

> During an interview with Sen. Ben Sasse, R-Neb., about his new book, *The Vanishing American Adult*,

Maher and Sasse were discussing adults who dress up for Halloween. Sasse said that happened less often in Nebraska, where the practice is "frowned upon."

"I've got to get to Nebraska more," said Maher.

To which Sasse earnestly replied, "You're welcome. We'd love to have you work in the fields with us."

Maher narrowed his brow. "Work in the fields?" he said, raising his palms. "Senator, I'm a house [N-word]?"

Sasse smiled uncomfortably, and some groans were audible from the audience. "It's a joke," protested Maher, moving the conversation along. Claps could then be heard from the audience.[68]

Whoa. Joke or not, obviously the use of this word in any context is entirely unacceptable. We can all agree that this word has a long history of animus and abuse that makes it very hurtful. There was certainly some backlash against Mr. Maher for using it. But the backlash was swift and quiet. The entire incident was essentially swept under the rug. Maher was not fired, and his show was not canceled.

Now, let's look at a second example. On May 29th, 2018, Roseanne Barr tweeted the following comment: "Muslim brotherhood & planet of the apes had a baby=vj."[69]

Objectively, the comment is somewhat ambiguous. I'm certainly not condoning it; however, I don't think it rises to the same level of abhorrence as Maher's overtly racist remark. Even giving both Maher and Barr the benefit of the doubt, there is no context in which Maher's comment would be acceptable. Yet, the backlash against Barr was immediate and extreme. She was labeled a racist, and her comment made national headlines and became a political talking point for weeks, if not longer. Barr was fired and her show was canceled.

How do we reconcile the dichotomy between how Bill Maher and Roseanne Barr were treated?

Let's look at some of the basic facts for a moment. According to Barr, she made the comment after she had mixed Ambien with alcohol. Let's give her the benefit of the doubt and assume that's true. Let's also assume that Barr suffers from clinical depression and sustained a traumatic brain injury when she was younger, which she also claims, and that she didn't know that Valerie Jarret was black. I think that any one of these facts alone demonstrates that Barr's comments were probably not malicious and at the very least that deserves a second chance.

I want to make it clear that I'm in no way defending Barr's comment or taking sides. I'm simply demonstrating the hypocrisy of the situation—how two similarly situated public figures are treated disparately, for what seems to be no other reason than their political affiliations. This is a prime example of the hysteria that has consumed our culture. We're far too easily "triggered" (the word alone "triggers" *me*). Logical thinking often goes out the window. As a result, many of us suppress our true opinions because we fear that we, too, might be labeled as some type of bigot. This paranoia has a chilling effect on speech and stifles progress. It's something we would expect in a dystopic, Orwellian society, not in our beautiful constitutional republic.

The current status of our public discourse makes it difficult to feel safe in public. It's like everyone is walking on eggshells all the time. And if you're not, then you probably should be. Apparently, a single misstep, no matter how innocuous, could ruin your life or your entire career. A person's true motivations are irrelevant. There is zero tolerance and zero forgiveness. This is particularly true if you are a public figure. Social media only makes the pressure more intense. It's suffocating and it's constant.

This is why I often get disheartened when I watch the news. I'm sure this is the case for many of you, as it can often be an overwhelming experience. It's constantly just so…negative. Sometimes, I even take a short hiatus just to preserve my psychological well-being. It feels like every day another notable figure says something that's considered "offensive." It's cyclical: the public is outraged; we demand blood (e.g., the person should be ridiculed or fired or forced to resign); the person apologizes;

the person is either spared, further castigated, or placed in limbo (hidden until the public forgets).

I'm going to go out on a limb here and venture a guess that each of us has also said things we wish we hadn't. Let's not forget that. Let's not hold others to a higher standard than we hold ourselves. We all make mistakes and will continue to make mistakes as long as we're alive. Heck, that's what humans do best—screw up! So, let's not only lighten up but let's also learn to forgive.

We've become so blind to our hypocrisy. We sit in our ivory towers and criticize countries like China for censoring access to information—for censoring entertainment and art—yet this is exactly what we are doing right here! Social media platforms like Facebook and YouTube have been blocking access to information and unilaterally purging the accounts of countless people based on criteria that are nebulous at best. The idea is that if you don't conform to the accepted social narrative, you will be erased. Independent thought is no longer allowed. Even entertainment—works of fiction—are being diluted by these politics. Entertainers are being admonished for their art. Either toe the line or face retribution.

Let's Alter Our Perspective

There's no doubt that this world is tough. We look for happiness, search for meaning, and seek truth. But let's try to recognize that no matter how someone's life appears, most of us are battling these same struggles, just to different degrees. Let's be mindful of this metaphysical connection—of our shared consciousness. Let's use these opportunities to educate, not eradicate.

Let's take a step even further back. Think about how fortunate you are to be reading these words. Not because they're so brilliant, but because you *can* read. You have access to books. You have money to spend. You have time to think about more than just basic survival. You might be hungry right now, but you're probably not worried about your next meal. You have a home. You have heat, electricity, water, drawers full of clothing. It might not be fancy, but you have it. You have the luxury of knowing what boredom is. You can spend time searching for a deeper understanding of life. You vacation. You dine. You have options.

I say this to provide perspective. In our consumer-driven culture, it's too easy to see the things we don't have rather than being mindful of what we do have. This is why it's important to be cognizant of what matters. Certainly, it's okay to want and have nice things. But we must recognize that things are exactly that: *things*.

Think about the deplorable conditions that so much of our world is forced to endure. Consider what these people would give to have just a fraction of what we have. Now think about the things that we obsess over. We are upset when a celebrity—an *entertainer*—says something that we disagree with or that we find offensive.

What if, instead of focusing on all of the superficial things that make us different, we focus on how we are the same.

Let's shut down our minds and take a deep breath. Block out all the external noises. Quiet that little voice that lives inside each of our heads. Now, think about who and *what* you are at the core of your being. Consider how a tweet from Kanye West affects *your* life. Think about whether the outcome of last night's baseball game truly affects *your* life. How having the newest iPhone model truly impacts your existence on this planet.

Consider the reason why you get up and go to work every day. Most of us work purely for survival. We work so that we can feed ourselves and our families, so that we can have stuff. And having stuff is okay. But having stuff doesn't necessarily make us happy. Of course, not having stuff won't necessarily make us happy either, but the point is that stuff alone isn't what provides happiness and isn't what makes us better people. Having stuff simply allows us to be comfortable. It gives us more time to do more of the things we enjoy doing. But, at the end of the day, it's just stuff. You can have all the stuff in the world, but without any meaningful relationships, life loses its meaning. That's because relationships are the foundation of life. Relationships create sustenance, empowerment, and fulfillment. Relationships are the cornerstone of everything we hold precious. This is often forgotten.

Now let's take another step back. Let's reassess our priorities. Sure, it's great to have material possessions, but let's be mindful of *why* we want these things.

When we leave this incarnation, we are left only with souls—a database of memories and experiences. These memories and experiences are what allows our souls to learn and grow. The stuff we own, although it might play a role in these memories, is purely tangential. The experiences we have, however, are what shape our memories. These memories become *who* we are, which in turn, shapes the "personality" of our souls from one incarnation to the next.

Every Interaction Matters

Every person on this planet has intrinsic value. Sometimes, we are so caught up in ourselves that we forget the value that others can add to our lives, even strangers. Almost all of my best experiences have resulted from interactions with others. Rarely do we experience true happiness from a solitary experience. Nor can a truly meaningful exchange be purely one-sided. Our everyday interactions shape our perspectives and help define who we are. Even the most ostensibly insignificant interactions add value to our lives.

When was the last time you started a conversation with a stranger?

Perhaps this is a silly question to those who live outside of New York City (my home), where most people I know actively seek to avoid such interactions. There are certainly other places I've traveled to where it's fairly common to strike up a conversation with a random stranger. But not here. This is understandable, though, in light of the overwhelming number of people here. Maybe it's the same in many other big cities, too. The stress of living amongst millions of other people in such a confined space can be daunting at times. We become hypervigilant, jaded, and distrustful of others. We isolate ourselves in public to protect against potential threats. But some of the most interesting and rewarding conversations I've ever had have been those that occurred unexpectedly with total strangers.

I was recently at dinner with a friend. It was a Friday night around 9 p.m. This is prime time in Manhattan. We were seated at a small, two-person table that was attached to another two-person table. We were eating in a tiny, nondescript Korean restaurant. In the center of the two tables was a removable divider. My friend and I sat at the table to the right, pressed against a wall. My back was facing the entrance and my friend was facing me. Next to my friend, a man was sitting alone. I could see his face, but it was somewhat obscured by the divider. My friend and I began talking.

When the waitress approached, we inquired about several items on the menu, at which point, the man chimed in and offered his opinion about a few things. Certainly, an unusual occurrence for New York. So, when the waitress walked away, the man apologized for interrupting our meal. Instead of simply accepting this man's unnecessary apology, I recognized an opportunity. It was Friday night, and this man was eating dinner alone. As a native New Yorker, one develops a knack for recognizing visitors, and I suspected that this man fit the bill. Either way, he was eating alone on a Friday night and would probably enjoy the company. So, I removed the divider that was between our tables and insisted that he join our meal.

For the next two hours, my friend and I spoke to this man, sharing our life stories. It turns out that I was right. He was visiting from Seattle to accept an award for his business and give a speech. It was very rewarding to vicariously share in the man's success. He was grateful for the company and we were grateful for the insights. This would never have happened if we had been unwilling to leave our comfort zones and explore the unknown. These types of interactions enhance our connection to and understanding of humanity. Despite our different backgrounds and superficial differences, we were able to bond with a total stranger and share in his celebration. For this brief time, the three of us were like family and transcended the hereditary boundaries that typically define this term. This is the essence of oneness.

I hope you now understand the importance of finding and living your truth. Being honest about your priorities and beliefs, and being confident in your decisions will help pave a smooth foundation on your path toward a spiritual purpose. By keeping a positive perspective in the face of adversity and embracing new challenges, your struggles will only serve to enhance your spiritual growth. We can also experience surprising shifts by keeping an open mind, being tolerant of differing opinions, and maintaining a strong sense of empathy and compassion.

CHAPTER 7

FORGIVENESS AND KARMA

Forgiveness

What is forgiveness?

This is a seemingly simple question with a seemingly straightforward answer. We often think of forgiveness in the context of anger or sadness. Usually, forgiveness arises when somebody has done something to hurt us and we move past it. Forgiveness usually means that although we have suffered as a result of someone else's actions, we are now able to accept what has happened.

Let's analyze forgiveness through a spiritual lens and revisit a concept we talked about earlier. Let's assume that we're all energy and that our actions create energetic responses, thereby creating inertia. The resultant energy would either be positive or negative, depending on the circumstances. A person who causes pain to another person has elicited a negative response in their counterpart. In turn, because energy must remain balanced, the person who caused the harm will also have elicited a negative response toward themselves.

According to the Law of One, this is the concept of karma.[70] Simplistically, what goes around comes around. The Law of One describes karma as simply balanced inertia. The idea that "those actions which are put into motion will continue using the ways of balancing until such time as the controlling or higher principle which you may liken unto your braking or stopping is invoked. This stoppage of the inertia of action may be called forgiveness. These two concepts are inseparable." Karma is the universe's way of maintaining order and balance.

Some of us have a very large capacity to forgive, while others may have nearly none. So, along with forgiveness are the notions of grudges, regrets, vengeance, and vindication. Those who are unable to forgive will often hold grudges and some of these grudges may even lead to thoughts of vengeance. "Getting even" is the idea that the person who hurt us deserves to be hurt in return, either directly or indirectly. But sometimes an act of revenge can be more severe than the original act. These acts can sometimes backfire and hurt innocent people, either physically or emotionally. Sometimes not.

Either way, vengeance is probably one of the most primal yet counterproductive measures we can take. Vengeance is purely visceral and serves no value other than to placate our ego. Some might argue that vengeance equates to fairness or justice. But I think this reasoning is flawed; it's just like saying that two wrongs equal a right. Not every misdeed warrants a punishment, and not every punishment fits the misdeed.

Of course, certain acts warrant punishment. I'm certainly not suggesting that we should never be held accountable for our actions or that people should never be penalized for their transgressions. But perhaps we need to rethink *how* and *why* we punish. The act of punishing, alone, without any rehabilitative component will only cause resentment, anger, and frustration. I think that often our desire for retribution stems from our inability to forgive.

Sure, it can feel good to inflict pain on someone who has caused you or someone you love pain. But this pleasure is usually short-lived and accompanied by guilt. Innately, most of us don't want to hurt other people. It goes against our better nature, even when we feel justified. In all likelihood, unless the person who wronged us is a psychopath or completely unaware of what they did, they probably have some sense of remorse for their actions. Most of us don't want to hurt other people. This is why the idea of holding a grudge or seeking vengeance is circular and will ultimately lead to regret.

So, how can we avoid this in the first place?

We all make mistakes. We have all, whether intentionally or not, done something to hurt or offend someone else. We are imperfect creatures. If we didn't make mistakes, then life would lose much of its meaning since we would have nothing to learn. Some mistakes are bigger than others, and our capacity to forgive usually depends on the severity of the circumstances. A minor lie from someone is certainly easier to forgive than an act of violence.

In some ways, I believe that our inability to forgive others stems from a lack of empathy. Once we place ourselves in another person's shoes, we have a better understanding of why that person has acted in a certain way. We might not agree with how the person acted and their actions might still cause us pain, but a sense of empathy allows for better insight into that person's mind, making their actions far easier to forgive. So, to experience empathy, we must be introspective. This is because if we want to truly understand the feelings of another, we must first understand our feelings. We have to identify where our desires, motivations, emotions, and perceptions stem from.

Forgiveness and the Law of One

As we just saw, the Law of One perceives forgiveness and karma as two inseparable concepts. Let's explore how this works.

We all expect that our actions will have consequences in the physical world. For example, if we break the law, we understand that we could get arrested and go to jail. But what happens on a metaphysical level when our actions hurt others? Remember, for every action, there is an equal and opposite reaction.[71] Karma is something that affects every single human being on Earth. Karma operates cyclically, creating patterns of energy and representing the connection between all things. Karma demonstrates how our actions affect not just ourselves, but everyone around us.

According to the Law of One, we can actually eliminate these negative patterns by simply being more understanding, accepting, and forgiving.[72] This just means that we need to be more empathetic toward those whom we affect by our actions, as well as toward ourselves.

But before we can truly learn to forgive others, we must first learn to forgive ourselves.[73] This might sound like a strange concept, but by forgiving oneself and never again making that same mistake, one can stop the wheel of karma.[74] This is because forgiveness of others is also forgiveness of self.[75] Of course, this isn't always so easy. As human beings, we have emotions (well, most of us). We have regrets about things we've done, regrets about things we didn't do, regrets about our relationships, careers, and a multitude of other things. We sometimes replay mistakes over and over in our minds or we act out how things could have gone differently. We convince ourselves that had we acted differently, we would have achieved a far more desirable outcome. We hold onto the "what ifs" and the "if onlys" until these feelings manifest into disappointments and missed opportunities.

It's far too easy to lose sight of the fact that the true value of our mistakes comes in the form of the lessons we learn. It's easy to blame ourselves and others when things don't go exactly as planned. I find the most effective solution is to embrace my mistakes instead of dwelling on them (although it's sometimes much easier said than done). For example, instead of dwelling on my unsuccessful past relationships, I'm grateful for the opportunities they provided to learn, grow, and become a better partner in my current relationship. Above all, my mistakes have led me to find my soulmate and have brought me to this very moment.

So, perhaps instead of referring to our unsuccessful endeavors as "failures" or "mistakes," we should simply call them lessons. It's easy to speculate about how things would have turned out if we had only made different decisions along the way. But we never *really* know, do we?

We never truly know how the decisions we make will ultimately impact our lives. This means that there is no such thing as a "wrong" decision; rather, there is only the decision that we made. It's all about altering our perspectives. So, if a decision has a less than desirable outcome, we can simply chalk it up to a learning experience that will better guide our future decisions toward a more desirable result. Every decision we make is the one that we were supposed to make because we made it using our free will. Just as our teachers in grade school used to tell us that there are no stupid questions, in our school called Earth, there are no wrong decisions.

This is not to say that we shouldn't feel guilty after we hurt someone else. But this is not the type of regret I'm talking about. I think that feelings of guilt are essential and coincide directly with our ability to empathize. It's what allows us to recognize that what we have done is immoral, that it was a decision we don't want to make again. It's what allows us to learn so that we don't repeat these actions. This is what I'll refer to as "short-term regret."

The type of regret that I think we should avoid is the "long-term regret"—those feelings that become obsessions. It's far too easy to dwell on our own perceived mistakes. Instead of using them as learning experiences, we sometimes harbor feelings of resentment toward ourselves or we blame others for our perceived shortcomings. This inhibits our spiritual progress because it perpetuates feelings of resentment, anger, and negativity. This negativity diverts our learning potential and nullifies the lessons that we could otherwise learn from. Instead of embracing the discomfort of our mistakes, we obsess over what we see as missed opportunities. The irony is that the real missed opportunities are not only the superficial lessons but also the deeper, spiritual lessons.

Let's think about it like this: what good does it serve us to obsess over our mistakes? To hold onto the negativity associated with an outcome that we perceive to be less than ideal? If anything, it makes us hypersensitive and overanalytical about every decision we make. This can thwart progress and create indecision. It can have a chilling effect on our success. It's a form of self-sabotage. Maybe we even begin to feel sorry for ourselves or become jealous or resentful of other people's successes.

We tell ourselves that we are just as capable as these other people. We are just as educated. Just as smart. So why can't *I* catch a break?

From an energetic perspective, these negative thoughts create negative energy. By dwelling on these negative thoughts, we are simply perpetuating this negativity, which in turn just attracts more negative energy. The negativity builds on itself and creates a negative spiral. It becomes circular. We begin putting out negative "vibes."

We all know someone who can shift the entire energy of the room when they walk in. Suddenly, everyone's mood changes. This can work in both a positive and negative sense. The person doesn't even need to speak, but maybe you feel anxious, depressed, or uncomfortable. It's like when we get a "creepy vibe" about someone. We know that something's off. We may comment that this person has a negative vibe.

On the other hand, some people can uplift the spirits of an entire room. They exude positivity. We are drawn to these people and enjoy just being in their presence. We may not be able to even articulate the reason, but we walk away thinking, "Wow, I really like that person!"

Why is this?

Some people balk at the idea that there is a metaphysical explanation for this. But I think it's as simple as the type of energy we exude. For me, I try to exude positivity as often as I can. I think this has had a demonstrable impact on my relationships and reputation with others. It has helped me both personally and professionally. I think I've always recognized that nobody wants to be around a negative person. Plus, it feels really good to be nice!

Accountability

Along with forgiveness comes the concept of accountability. We cannot genuinely forgive ourselves unless we can take accountability for our actions. Nor can we expect others to forgive our actions if we are not truly sorry for what we've done. I think that many of us have a problem taking accountability for our actions. We often convince ourselves that our actions were justified. Even when we know that someone was hurt by what we've done, we make excuses. We get defensive. We tell ourselves that the other person is overly sensitive or deserved what happened to them.

But here's the thing: even if we earnestly believe that our actions were justified, if our actions hurt someone, then perhaps we should take a step back and try to view the situation objectively. As cliché as this is, I try to put myself in the other person's shoes, imagining what it must feel like to be them. I ask myself how the other person may have perceived my words, my tone, the pitch and decibel of my voice. I try to separate myself from what my intentions were and eliminate my ego. I try to be as neutral as possible. I ask myself whether it is reasonable that what I said or did could have been misperceived, even if it was the opposite of my intentions. More often than not, the answer is yes.

Accountability goes hand in hand with the concept of compromise. All successful relationships, whether it be with a partner, family member, friend, coworker, etcetera, require some level of compromise. Nobody is perfect or right all the time. There is always room for compromise. Being empathetic enables us to be better at approaching compromise. By doing so, we are acknowledging our potential to make mistakes. We are acknowledging that sometimes our best intentions fail.

I would like to think that most of us rarely have malicious intentions and that most of the arguments we have stem from misunderstandings. We can't expect to avoid all misunderstandings, but we can try to prevent the arguments from spiraling out of control in the first place.

I have learned that instead of arguing, the best approach is to simply have a conversation. Instead of becoming defensive, I try to understand how my actions could have been perceived and how my actions could have affected the other person. Instead of trying to justify myself, I'll often begin with an apology: "I'm so sorry I hurt you." This means setting aside my ego and remaining completely objective.

Then, and only then, can we explain (not justify) our actions. We can explain that we never intended to cause them harm. We can explain what our intentions were to provide context for our words and actions. This will also help avoid future misunderstandings. Lastly, we should articulate our empathy. We should explain that in retrospect, we understand why the other person might feel the way they do, and that we understand how our words or actions may have affected that person in the way that they did.

Accountability doesn't mean that we must apologize unequivocally and without consideration. But it does require that we exhibit empathy and patience toward others.

Freeing Ourselves and Growing Our Souls

Let's explore how the concept of reincarnation fits into all this. Although many mainstream religions believe in reincarnation, it is rarely ever spoken about. The subject seems almost taboo. But reincarnation is something that is discussed in detail at various points throughout the Law of One.

I like to think of reincarnation as a pathway to advance our spiritual evolution similar to the way that our physical bodies advance during each lifetime. According to the Law of One, the very first time our souls inhabit a physical body we are born into a state of spiritual darkness.[76] We forget and are unable to access our spiritual roots. But this confusion is necessary because it enables us to evolve and learn lessons through the use of free will.

At the very beginning of our incarnation process, although we are quite innocent, we still have animalistic instincts. We are spiritually primitive, focused mostly on our survival. We view others more selfishly—as a means for self-preservation. But as we repeat the cycles of incarnation, we become aware that our needs extend beyond our mere survival. We begin to yearn for intangible things like companionship, laughter, and beauty. We develop the need to know and understand the universe.

As we begin to accumulate incarnations, our needs become more outwardly focused. We discover a need to trade; to love and to be loved; to elevate our animalistic behaviors to a more universal perspective. Ultimately, as our souls develop, we begin to focus more and more of each incarnation on the lessons of love. The more we experience in each lifetime, the more necessary it becomes to review these lessons once our physical lives end. This allows us to review where we went right, where we went wrong, and heal some of the emotional trauma we sustained. These experiences help us determine the parameters of our next incarnation. This is why at the beginning of the book, I said that there are very few coincidences in life. We choose to place ourselves in certain situations so that we can learn the lessons that we feel are necessary to learn. Nothing is by chance.

Sometimes, when I am going through a particularly rough patch, I try to remind myself of this. It doesn't always make things easier, but it usually helps put things in perspective. I try to find the lessons and how I can use them to benefit me in the future. I remind myself that the stress is never permanent and often results from me worrying about what *could* happen instead of what *will* happen. This is also why I always try to remain as positive as possible because I believe that positivity attracts more positivity. This has proven itself to be true for me time and again. But the inverse is also true. One of the things that helps me overcome my feelings of stress and anxiety is to have a goal and work toward that goal. I don't always map out every step or have a precise plan, but I never allow myself to lose sight of my ultimate objective. I take it step by step, day by day, moment by moment. We are each responsible for our destiny.

I understand that it can be hard to imagine that we would choose to place ourselves in unpleasant situations. After all, if we have a choice, why would we not just choose the easy path and make life simple? Well, I think that if we always choose the easy route, then we would never have anything to learn. Some of my most significant learning experiences have resulted from my greatest struggles. I have learned that it sometimes takes being in the trenches—where I feel beaten and worn down—before I can truly learn anything.

We predetermine many of the fundamental structures of our lives. These are things like our parents, family, friends, relationships, and occupations. This also means that the people in our lives also choose us. Everything is intertwined and connected like a gigantic, metaphysical spiderweb. Think about it for a minute. Have you ever met someone that you immediately connected with? Maybe you can't even explain why, but you instantly took a liking to this person. Perhaps it even blossomed into a strong friendship or a romantic relationship.

It's all too easy to dismiss these things as coincidences. Sometimes, I resist the idea that certain things are "meant to be" because it forces me to relinquish some level of control over my life. This is not to say I don't believe we always have a choice. But I think there are certain decisions we are "supposed" to make and failing to do so will prevent us from fulfilling at least a part of what we hoped to. This is not always easy to accept, particularly when bad things happen. These types of events force me to reconsider my perspective. It requires that I step back from the situation I am dealing with and try to objectively assess what's happening. I have to remind myself that sometimes the lesson is beyond my current understanding. I can look back to some of the bad things that happened to me over a decade ago and understand why they were necessary. Although these events were stressful at the time, in retrospect, they were necessary for me to become the person I am today. The real rewards have always happened as a result of my struggles.

Even as I write these very words, I feel stressed about some upcoming deadlines at work, being prepared for the class I have to teach in a few hours, and meeting the deadline to submit my latest round of edits on this book by later tonight! This is true even though I believe that everything is happening precisely as I planned it. I understand that it's not always easy to just search for some hidden meaning and have faith that everything will work out how it is supposed to. Let's be real. Life is tough and all of this is much easier said than done. I can't simply ignore the stress and just have blind faith, or ignore logic and common sense. This concept is far easier to discuss in the abstract than it is to put into practice. Think about it—it's often very easy to offer advice to a friend when the answer seems clear, but when the situation is reversed and we are the ones seeking advice, the same simple answer can seem much more complicated.

We are only human, after all. We have emotions, priorities, and concerns. We can't avoid this. But I think that this is exactly how we learn. These experiences would be far less valuable if they were all pleasant. As natural as it is for me to be happy and excited, I believe it's equally as natural that I am sometimes stressed, anxious, or depressed. For me, the key to handling these negative emotions is to accept that I'm feeling a certain way and then assess the cause. I try very hard not to fight them. Instead, I ask myself why I feel this way and what actions I can take to change it. I accept that bad things sometimes happen, but I never accept that the bad things are permanent. I believe there's always a solution. It may not be the most pleasant option. It may not be easy. It may not be ideal. But a solution exists.

Think back to a situation when you overcame adversity. It's likely that at some point during your struggle, the situation seemed insurmountable. But you prevailed. Think about how you accomplished this goal. Maybe you were in a toxic relationship. You felt trapped. But you told yourself that this person was the best you were going to get. You found a million ways to justify staying in the relationship. You were together for such a long time that your family was their family and vice versa. This person knew you and they understood you in ways that seemed like nobody else could. The idea of having to find someone new seemed daunting. So, you stayed until one day you worked up enough courage to take the risk. And the very moment you did, your chest felt lighter; you could suddenly breathe more easily. You felt liberated. In retrospect, you begin to realize that you were always free. Yes, the relationship had been unpleasant, and the breakup was even worse, but the only person holding you back was yourself. You are, and always have been, the one in control.

I think the real paradox is trying to understand that we can simultaneously have free will and fate. I believe that we are incarnated with certain objectives and that although certain major events are predestined and will almost certainly occur regardless of the path we choose, the path we take to reach our objectives—and perhaps even the result itself—can have infinite variations. This means that we have charted out a certain course that we seek to take to reach specific goals. If we stay on course, we will achieve these goals using the path we charted. If we deviate off course, we may either achieve these goals, albeit using an alternate path, or fail to achieve them. I believe that we utilize subsequent incarnations to achieve unfulfilled goals.

I think two very poignant examples of deviating from our paths are suicide and murder. While death itself may be natural and charted, suicide and murder not only cut short the victim's intended life path, but these things also affect the countless other people the victim would have otherwise interacted with, creating a domino effect. It is the potentially infinite effect these acts have on others that I believe creates negative karma on the individual who perpetrates these acts, which will consequently follow them into subsequent lifetimes. I believe that some of us experience certain events in our current lives that are the direct result of things we did in our past lives. This is the idea of "working off" or balancing our karma.

This is also the reason I think the idea that any of us will suffer some sort of eternal damnation for the mistakes we make in any given lifetime is pretty absurd. Yet the concept of heaven and hell is something that facilitates the lives of tens of millions of people worldwide. Some believe that things like religion, sexual orientation, music, and clothing each determine our afterlife. But if you're anything like me, then these trivialities will seem just a little bit too extreme to digest. I think these are the very types of beliefs that push many of us away from traditional religion in the first place.

Each of us has a different moral barometer. Each of us is born under a different set of circumstances. We have different upbringings, experiences, and influences in our lives. Each of these things affects each of us differently. For example, I think that most of us would agree that stealing is wrong. But even something so seemingly straightforward could depend on the circumstances. There's a huge difference between a person who steals a loaf of bread to survive and a person who steals for purely superficial reasons. So, determining what's right and wrong might not always be so clear. That said, it would be difficult for any single factor to be entirely determinative of our afterlife. There are just far too many variables for bright-line rules to make any sense.

I think most of us would also agree that each of us would benefit from living positive and virtuous lives. It only makes sense to me that acts of love and compassion will allow our souls to grow and evolve. The idea that our souls undergo an evolution is incompatible with the notion that we live only a single incarnation, which then determines where we will spend the remainder of eternity. This is not to say that it's incompatible with the concept of an afterlife, generally a nonphysical realm where our souls reconnect to the original source and reflect on our experiences before we begin our next incarnation. This would mean that to evolve—to learn—our souls would need to incarnate many times. A single finite life can't teach us everything we need to know. I think it makes much more sense that we live many lives, each of which is focused on a particular goal or set of goals. We then experience a similar set of circumstances during a different incarnation until we learn whatever lessons we intend to learn before moving onto different objectives.

As I alluded to before, the idea of experiencing multiple incarnations and a multitude of experiences goes hand in hand with the concept of karma. Because karma is essentially inertia or the universe's way of maintaining order and balance, we can build up more karma during a particular incarnation than we can "burn off" or balance. So, additional incarnations would be required to achieve order and balance. This also helps to explain why sometimes we experience struggles in our lives even when it may seem unjustified. I think this also explains our creation of the heaven and hell concepts, as these are most likely distortions resulting from our misapprehensions of karma and reincarnation.

Although one could argue that there is no tangible proof for what I'm saying—which is no different than any religious or spiritual concept—there have been many documented cases of people who remember living an entirely different life before their current incarnation. Some of these people even carry certain trauma (e.g., anxiety and phobias) into their current lives that resulted from something that occurred in a prior one.

An excellent example of this is a book written by a Yale-educated psychiatrist named Dr. Brian Weiss, entitled *Many Lives, Many Masters*. Dr. Weiss begins by explaining that he had trained for many years to think like a scientist and physician. This made him skeptical of anything that could not be proven by traditional scientific methods, which makes his findings all the more interesting.[77] All of this changed one day when he met Catherine, whom he used conventional methods of therapy on for eighteen months to help her overcome her symptoms. When none of these methods worked, he tried hypnosis. The results were nothing short of astonishing. According to Dr. Weiss, during "a series of trance states, Catherine recalled 'past-life' memories that proved to be the causative factors of her symptoms. She also was able to act as a conduit for information from highly evolved 'spirit entities,' [whom he refers to as "Masters"] and through them, she revealed many of the secrets of life and death. In just a few short months, her symptoms disappeared, and she resumed her life, happier and more at peace than ever before."

During one of the sessions, Catherine, while under hypnosis, had just finished discussing a death in a past life and then made an interesting comment that she was "resting, after death, in between lifetimes." After several minutes of silence,

Catherine spoke again, only her voice had now changed. When she spoke, Catherine said, "our task is to learn, to become God-like through knowledge. We know so little. You are here to be my teacher. I have so much to learn. By knowledge we approach God, and then we can rest. Then we come back to teach and help others."

Catherine's comments highlight a theme we've been discussing throughout this book: we are all here to both learn and teach. I believe the experience and knowledge we gain during our prior lives are embedded within our cellular memory and help guide us in our current lives. So, we have much to learn but also much to teach, utilizing our experiences from all lifetimes.

In his book, Dr. Weiss acknowledges that nothing in his background had prepared him for this and that he was "absolutely amazed" when this occurred. He also admits that there is no scientific explanation for what happened. Dr. Weiss hypothesizes that maybe Catherine, while under hypnosis, was able to access the part of her subconscious mind that stores authentic past-life memories, "or perhaps she had tapped into what the psychoanalyst Carl Jung termed the collective unconscious, the energy source that surrounds us and contains the memories of the entire human race."

Truly remarkable! Dr. Weiss had accidentally stumbled upon a metaphysical overlap in his psychiatric work. To his credit, instead of dismissing these occurrences outright (as it seems many scientists do), he followed them down the rabbit hole. Dr. Weiss struggled—and perhaps still struggles—with the parts of his findings that cannot be proven or explained by any conventional scientific method. Interestingly, Dr. Weiss also references the work of Carl Jung and his notion of a collective unconscious, which we discussed earlier, although he takes it a step further by accepting the possibility that Catherine's past-life memories were authentic. Also interesting is what Dr. Weiss describes as "highly evolved 'spirit entities,'" who communicated and conveyed information of a spiritual nature to Catherine. This is a direct parallel to the Law of One in which a higher source of intelligence spoke through Carla Rueckert while she, just like Catherine, was in a trance-like state. What's more, Dr. Weiss notes that some of the information Catherine provided was particularly inexplicable (and psychic in nature), such as references to and knowledge of specific events in his past, his father, and his children. Again, to his credit, Dr. Weiss does not dismiss the potential authenticity of these spiritual entities or the veracity of the information they provided to Catherine. Dr. Weiss goes out of his way to preface the book by stating that as a psychiatrist and scientist, he is naturally skeptical and far from naïve. Yet even he had to accept the possibility—and perhaps likelihood—that the information being provided by and to Catherine was genuine.

It's also important to remember that Dr. Weiss has treated thousands of patients and runs four major inpatient psychiatric hospitals. He is an expert in his field and has the skills and training necessary to detect fraudulent and sociopathic behavior. Catherine exhibited none of these characteristics. Dr. Weiss ultimately acknowledges that Catherine's knowledge of historical events and other facts was simply far too accurate and precise to be disingenuous. He even goes so far as to dismiss alternative scientific explanations for Catherine's past-life memories, such as "genetic memory," which would entail the unbroken passage of genetic material from generation-to-generation. This is because Catherine's past lives occurred all over the world, resulting in her genetic line being repeatedly interrupted, terminating her genetic pool and preventing its transmission. Yet Catherine's memories continued, even in the absence of a body and genetic material.

According to Dr. Weiss, exploring our past lives through regression therapy can have a much more powerful curative effect than conventional therapy or even modern medicine. This is an incredibly bold statement for a respected medical doctor to make because it defies conventional treatment and is certain to expose him to a barrage of assaults from the medical community. Yet Dr. Weiss claims that the force of remembering and reliving both traumatic past-life events and everyday insults to the mind, body, and ego was similar to conventional therapy and helped cure psychiatric ailments with tremendous rapidity. This was true not only of Catherine but of Dr. Weiss's later patients as well.

Dr. Weiss's book is important for many reasons. One is that it yet again proves a direct correlation between science and spirituality. Dr. Weiss addresses two very interesting spiritual topics that relate directly to this book. The first is the concept of reincarnation. The second is the notion that Catherine conveyed genuine spiritual information from a higher source of intelligence, just like in the Law of One. I also think Dr. Weiss, a reputable psychiatrist, was quite courageous in publishing his findings and opinions regarding his past-life regression studies, as doing so is largely taboo. Dr. Weiss acknowledges these risks and explains that scientists are only just beginning to seek the answers to the seemingly inexplicable anomalies that the human mind is capable of. He also discusses the inherent struggle of science to accept new and ostensibly esoteric concepts. He explains that a prime example of this is the refusal of many in the medical field to accept the "considerable evidence" about death, the afterlife, and reincarnation. Lastly, I think Dr. Weiss's book is important to highlight the benefits of holistic medical practices and alternative (non-pharmaceutical) forms of therapy.

Hopefully, you now understand why forgiveness is the linchpin of spiritual growth. Through forgiving ourselves and forgiving others, you can eliminate the negative patterns that create bad karma and hinder your progress from one incarnation to the next.

CHAPTER 8

SYNCHRONICITY

I was first inspired to write this chapter early one morning while standing on a subway platform waiting for the train to arrive. I had been writing this book for a while but wasn't quite sure what I wanted to write about that day. As I waited, I was listening to a podcast when it suddenly froze. I looked down at the screen on my phone and noticed the time of the podcast said 1:13:13. When I got onto the train, I noticed that the number on the subway car was 2222. Finally, when I arrived at my office to start writing and looked at the clock, the time was 8:13. Okay, I thought to myself, today I'm going to write about synchronicity: instances of seemingly random coincidences that appear to coordinate with incredible precision and frequency in our lives.

But first, a little background. I was born on August 13th, so the numbers eight and thirteen have always held a lot of significance for me. I find these numbers repeatedly appearing in my life in many different forms. With shocking regularity, I will decide to check the time and it just so happens to be 8:13. In some instances, it will be the first time I checked the time in hours, yet there it is. Other times, I'll make a purchase and the receipt will be for $8.13 or $13.13 or some other variation of these numbers. Many people would merely shrug off these occurrences as coincidences or maybe not even notice them at all. But I think there's something more at play. Something with a greater cosmic significance.

When I discuss spirituality with other people, many different topics often arise. People share stories about unexplained phenomena that have happened in their lives. Maybe it's a prophetic or vivid dream where someone receives a helpful message or is visited by a deceased family member or friend. Other times, it can be a series of seemingly random coincidences that protects someone from misfortune or tragedy. Many of us have heard stories from a parent or grandparent where they swear that they experienced an unusually clairvoyant event. Whatever the occurrence, most of us have been exposed to spirituality or even the paranormal in one way or another. I certainly understand the reluctance to discuss these things because we've been conditioned to be skeptical of anything that doesn't conform to our preconceived set of rules. We demand to see the evidence and when no evidence appears, we become critical.

But I think it's important to remember that the absence of evidence is not the evidence of absence. Sometimes, an ostensible lack of evidence simply means that we need to look more closely and connect the dots. Think about how law enforcement officers solve crimes. In most cases, the evidence isn't always cut and dry. There's rarely a smoking gun that instantly solves the case. But this doesn't mean there's no evidence at all. Most crimes are solved by utilizing circumstantial evidence, or fitting together little pieces of evidence like pieces of a puzzle. Think about how important DNA evidence has become to solving crimes. DNA evidence was a relatively unknown concept before we discovered ways to detect and test for it. Now it's become the norm and we accept its accuracy, even though it's invisible to our naked eye. We all understand that DNA is the fundamental building block of our physical bodies.

Now think about what would happen if science eventually found a way to detect the soul. Think about what this would mean for humanity. Suddenly, science would have to incorporate a spiritual explanation for theories about our existence. It would have to find a way for DNA to coexist with the soul. Just because we cannot detect the soul using any conventional scientific techniques does not mean the soul does not exist. Similarly, just because we may perceive that certain occurrences are merely coincidence or luck does not mean there isn't some hidden force guiding these occurrences. All we need to do is open our eyes and be aware.

I like to visualize the metaphysical world as the one-way mirror we see in all those police interrogation rooms on television. If you've ever watched a detective show, you know exactly what I'm talking about. Usually, someone is sitting at a table in an interrogation room and there's a mirror on the wall. On the other side of the mirror are detectives watching and listening through the glass. The detectives can see out but the suspect sitting in the interrogation room can't see back in. When the suspect looks in the mirror, they see only their reflection. But the suspect usually knows someone is watching on the other end. They are aware that the mirror is nothing more than an illusion. So, maybe our physical world is nothing more than an interrogation room separated from the metaphysical world by a one-way mirror. Perhaps there are entities on the other side of this mirror that not only watch and listen to us but also help and guide us toward our goals. Maybe there are even rules these entities have to follow, like a code of conduct, so they do not directly intervene and infringe on our free will. Perhaps they provide us with subtle clues to help remind us that they exist and are here to support us. Maybe we can even sense them at times.

Earlier, we discussed Carl Jung and his theory of the collective unconscious. Well, Jung's collective unconscious theory touches upon another metaphysical topic, a principle he termed "synchronicity." According to Jung, synchronicity is the occurrence of one or more seemingly unrelated events with no obvious causal connection.[78] To his credit, Jung refuses to accept the notion that these events are simply the product of "chance" or "coincidence." Instead, he opines that just because there isn't an obvious causality, doesn't mean it doesn't exist. The more logical explanation is that we simply haven't discovered it yet. Although Jung tacitly acknowledges that there can be hidden causal connections that exist metaphysically, he stubbornly refuses to acknowledge the spiritual implications these connections have and insists on labeling them empirical or scientific concepts. Jung states that synchronicity is neither materialism nor metaphysical. Instead, he views this concept as a quaternion supplement to the triad of classical physics' space, time, and causality. So, once again, Jung opts for a classical scientific explanation.

While we are on the topic of synchronicity, as I wrote these very words, I received a text from my fiancé about a dream she had. She told me that she dreamed she was dead and floating in a pool while watching her body from below. Creepy. When she texted me, I was reading a passage from Carl Jung's book *Synchronicity: An Acausal Connecting Principle* to help guide my writing. The passage discussed a story Jung was told by one of his patients who had gone into a coma after traumatic childbirth. The woman told him that she found herself looking down at her body from above and watching as the doctors, nurses, and members of her family frantically assessed the situation from below (just like my fiancé in her dream). As the woman floated, she was aware of a beautiful entrance to another world sitting just behind her. The woman awoke from her coma fifteen hours later and was able to describe in full detail what had transpired during her coma. Even Jung admits that the woman could not have been in a psychogenic twilight state (in which part of her consciousness continued to operate while she was seemingly unconscious) because her heart had collapsed, causing her to lose consciousness as a result of cerebral anemia. According to Jung, this should have led to a complete blackout, preventing any clear observation or sound judgment.

I decided to include this example in my book because of the synchronicity in the timing of my fiancé's text and its relevance to the topic of synchronicity. Jung believes that this type of occurrence is synchronistic because there is no causal connection to the usual organic processes. Although Jung struggles to find a scientific explanation for how these types of events could occur, he still discusses causation in the context of metaphysical phenomena, such as ESP, which he defines as "perceptions independent of space and time which cannot be explained as processes in the biological substrate." To explain phenomena like the one described before without incorporating any spiritual principles, Jung hypothesizes that there is likely just an unknown layer to our nervous system that is capable of producing and transmitting psychic processes.

Once again, we see that Jung treads a fine line between science and metaphysics without ever truly acknowledging the spiritual implications of his work. Maybe this is because certain spiritual concepts, like the soul, are amorphous and impossible to measure (at least using any conventional scientific methodologies). So, scientists like Jung would rather formulate a scientific theory (however tenuous) than give a metaphysical explanation, as doing so aligns better with their education and subjects them to far less scrutiny. After all, a metaphysical theory would require just as much speculation as one based on science, so why open Pandora's box?

Turning to a more metaphysical approach, as I alluded to earlier, synchronicities often appear in our lives in the form of repeating numbers, particularly those that are significant to us. I believe that these occurrences are subtle divine messages and try to be mindful of their occurrence. These types of synchronicities do not just occur as repeating numerical patterns but can take the form of many different types of ostensible "coincidences" throughout our lives. Most of us have experienced these events in some form or another, and some of us more than others. Think about a time when you were just sitting around thinking about someone you know (a brother, your mother, a friend, whomever), and then your phone buzzes. You look down and realize that the person you were just thinking about is calling or just sent a text.

These are the types of synchronicities that happen to us all the time. Maybe you've been struggling with a decision. You've been leaning in one direction but aren't entirely sure whether it's the right decision. Yet whenever you start thinking about your decision, the same song starts playing on the radio or you see the same sequence of numbers appear over and over again. These types of synchronicities could very well be messages that your instincts about the decision are correct. If we simply shrug them off or dismiss them as just random coincidences, we are losing valuable opportunities to recognize a potentially greater message.

So, who might be sending these messages and why?

I believe that these messages come from spirits who act as our guides and assist us as we move through life. Some people refer to these entities as their "spirit guides" or "guardian angels." I don't think there's any practical distinction. Here's a scenario: you're standing on a street corner with your face buried in your phone. You're about to take a step into the street but something nudges you to look up at the last second. Good thing you did because a car goes whizzing past in the exact location where you would have stepped. It's far too easy to simply move past these experiences without any real thought, but I think these little intuitive nudges are often more than just plain luck.

I've become much more attuned to these signals as I get older. When I was in my early twenties, I would sometimes need the universe to (almost quite literally) slap me in the face before I recognized that I was headed toward disaster. One very personal example occurred when I was nineteen years old. I had just returned to college to start my sophomore year. It was the first week of school. Classes had just started. I was now living off campus, and I was engaging in some reckless and self-destructive behavior. Suddenly, I found myself immersed in serious legal troubles. I was kicked out of school and had to petition them to allow me back in. To add insult to injury, just two days later, my foot was run over by a car.

So, there I was, on crutches, in pain, and facing significant legal issues. I had hit rock bottom. I quickly recognized that all of the bad things that were happening to me were messages that I had to change my lifestyle, or I would continue to spiral down this self-destructive path. Fortunately, I listened to these messages and cleaned up my act. I was able to resolve the legal problems, and everything ultimately worked out better than I could have even imagined. During these eight terrible months, instead of dwelling on the problems and feeling sorry for myself, I used this time to improve myself. This was the very point in time when I began my spiritual journey.

All of this is to say that I think synchronicity is a way of reminding us why we came here in the first place. It provides us with subtle affirmations to our doubts about life. Nobody is going to spoon-feed us all the answers. We have to get our hands a little dirty and fight in the trenches. That's why we're here. But synchronicities occur by giving us a thumbs-up when we're on the right path or a thumbs-down to help guide us back on track. I've noticed that once I began to recognize the signs and appreciate the synchronicities, they occur far more frequently and in some truly remarkable ways. This has also encouraged me to follow my instincts and pursue my truth. The positive affirmations I've received have made me more confident and have helped me overcome self-doubt. I now feel more confident taking risks and leaving my comfort zone.

I don't think there's a definitive way to recognizing synchronicities because it's all a very personal thing. In my experience, if I suspect something is a sign it usually proves itself to be a sign. If I'm uncertain, so long as I keep my eyes open, I usually see the sign repeat itself over and over again. Sometimes synchronicities will align almost in rapid succession as they did for me in my example above. I think that each of our guides is intimately attuned with who we are and understands our motivations and doubts better than anyone else (perhaps even better than ourselves). So, although the signs might be subtle, it seems that they're uniquely catered to our idiosyncrasies. We just need to be aware and keep ourselves open to receiving them.

I also think that how we interpret the signs is a uniquely personal thing. Like I said before, there are certain numbers and sequences of numbers that have meaning to me. But some numbers have universal meaning.

For example, the number three signifies having trust in the universe to provide us with truth and purpose in life. Maybe you've been having a difficult time at work lately and you continually see the number three popping up. This could very well be your guides telling you to have faith. I usually find that I see these numbers in multiples, like "333." For example, I'll check the time and notice it's 3:33 or I'll check my inbox and see I have 333 emails. If you're seeing the number three over and over again, it could be a sign telling you to have faith (seeing a single three) or a message that your guides are ready to help or that something you've been seeking is coming your way (seeing three consecutive threes in a row). Or maybe it's a variation of the above. I think the specific message depends on our unique set of circumstances.

Life is not just a series of random events or coincidences; rather, it's a set of methodically planned out lessons that we are guided toward through synchronicities. I think that if you look closely enough, you'll begin to see these signs permeating into your life in some truly remarkable ways. It was very powerful synchronicity that truly inspired me to finally buckle down and write this book.

About a year before I started writing this book in earnest, I was maybe a quarter of the way done writing the first draft. I had a vision. I had a goal. But I was filled with self-doubt and didn't have a disciplined writing routine. My fiancé knew that I was struggling and bought me a book called *Start Writing Your Book Today* by Morgan Gist MacDonald. The moment I opened the book, I was stunned. Morgan's introduction contained several lines that mirrored lines I had already written almost verbatim! As I read these opening lines, I immediately recognized this as an affirmation that I was on the right path. This was precisely the encouragement I needed to get more serious about my writing and finish the book. Morgan's book not only provided this affirmation, but it also provided me with the perfect strategy to finish my book.

But the synchronicities didn't end here. Just two days after opening Morgan's book, I had already finished it and was so excited that I decided to email her to thank her. I told her about the unusual synchronicities in our writing. When Morgan responded, she told me that she had started her own publishing company, the goal of which was to assist aspiring authors to reach their potential. As it happens, Morgan's company was in the process of accepting applicants for a new writing program geared toward helping aspiring authors publish their first book! The writing group also paired the writers up with an editor-coach who reviewed our work and provided useful feedback. This was *exactly* what I needed at *exactly* the right time. What better way to validate my writing than to have a series of synchronicities occur directly as a result of reading a book, the purpose of which was to help me write my book in the first place.

These synchronicities continued to occur as I wrote the book. Despite my confidence and belief in these synchronicities, I cannot always avoid the inevitable self-doubt from seeping through. As I was writing and experiencing a moment of self-doubt, I was inspired by another synchronicity. The synchronicity occurred after a very long and stressful day of work. After a nearly twelve-hour workday, I felt exhausted and overwhelmed but decided to do a little writing to help clear my mind. I was writing the portion about extraterrestrials and crop circles. I knew about the thirteen-mile-long crop circle in the desert appearing somewhere around 1991 but couldn't remember the name. I Googled "1991 crop circles dessert 13 mile long" (yes, I was tired and misspelled desert). When the results popped up, I was astonished. As you will see below, the very first search result that displayed on my screen was a YouTube video posted by someone with the username "goforitRANDY." This was a sign so obvious it nearly punched me in the face.

Take a look for yourself:

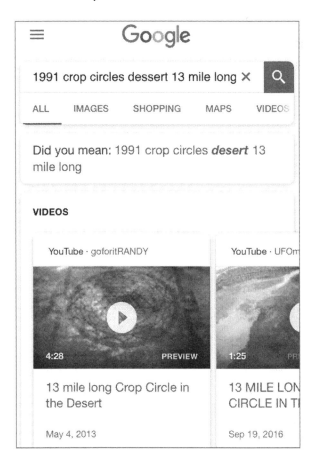

Just when I was feeling the lowest I'd felt in months, I received a message telling me, in no uncertain terms, to go for it! This was a truly humbling validation.

As I conclude this chapter, I'll leave you with a challenge. Be aware, open your eyes, and try to notice these types of signs around you. Instead of dismissing these occurrences as coincidence, stop and assess the situation. Focus on what you were thinking about in that moment and what is going on in your life. Are you struggling with a big decision? Are you simply seeking validation? Try to determine what the synchronicity could mean. I think your instincts are probably right. Most importantly, take note of how often your thoughts align with the reality around you.

CHAPTER 9

HARMONY, BALANCE, AND SYMBIOSIS

Finding Balance from Within

Being spiritual is not only about changing our mental outlook, but it's also about living a balanced and healthy lifestyle. It's about recognizing our mind-body-spirit connection. This means eating healthy, exercising, and meditating daily. After all, if our bodies aren't functioning optimally, then how can our minds? Plus, exercising and eating healthy makes us look and feel good. This will improve our mood, increase our confidence, and make us overall happier people. As we will soon discuss, adding meditation to the mix will help round out this trifecta of healthy living necessities.

Something truly powerful happens when a group of people comes together to support a common goal. There is a palpable energy that resonates. I used to live down the block from one of the routes of the New York City Marathon. Tens of thousands of people run this race, and tens of thousands of people also stand outside to support those running. People from all over the world line up behind metal police barricades for miles upon miles. Some are cheering on family and friends; others are cheering for total strangers. There are dozens of bands playing. There are DJs. There are hundreds of volunteers. Everyone wants to show their support.

Many of the runners write their names on their shirts so that people can cheer them on as they run. Nobody in the crowd has anything to gain by watching. They want to show their support, and their positivity helps motivate the runners to complete the race. You can see it in the runners' faces: the smiles, the nods of appreciation, the waves, the high fives. The crowd is equally entranced. When a disabled runner passes by, the crowd goes even wilder. This is such a beautiful thing.

The sad part is that it's such a rare occurrence. I think it's such a remarkable thing when we are all able to put aside our differences—even for just a short time—and come together to support one another. It is in these moments that we forget about what divides us. We forget about our individual identities and view ourselves as part of something greater: humanity. It feels so much better to love than to hate. These feelings are compounded when we're in a large group that has gathered for a positive purpose. I think the marathon is a good example because there is absolutely no pretext. Unless you're a professional runner, there are no real winners or losers. Everyone is out there to just do their best and finish the race. It's all about camaraderie.

On the contrary, many other types of large gatherings, like political rallies and professional sporting events, often have a polarizing effect. We want our candidate, our cause, our team to win. We advocate for our side and vocalize our negative feelings about our adversary. It's a mixture of both positive and negative emotions. I think that in these moments, our feeling of empowerment stems from a place of both love and hate. Overall, I believe this weakens the otherwise beneficial effect our positivity can have.

How do we strike a balance?

I think we can gain a lot of insight from nature. Think about the symbiosis that exists within a balanced and untainted ecosystem. This is analogous to our potential as human beings to achieve a state of peace and harmony. Now, think about the battle for self-preservation that exists within these ecosystems. These animalistic instincts mirror our behavior and provide insight into our destructive tendencies. Wild animals exist with a singular purpose: survival. For a species to survive, it must be able to eat and it must be able to reproduce. This often means survival of the fittest. This helps explain why most animals are so territorial and why they will resort to violence for even the most minor of breaches. Animals can't communicate the way we can, so they can't negotiate or compromise with one another. Humans, on the other hand, have enhanced cognitive and communicative abilities that obviate the need for violence to eat and reproduce. This should be a reminder that violent and territorial behavior is primitive and counterproductive.

When an animal is in its natural environment, it's part of a vast ecosystem where everything works together to maintain homeostasis. An incredible example of this symbiosis is marine cleaning stations. These are natural underwater locations where aquatic creatures congregate to be cleaned by smaller fish.[79] The most fascinating part about these cleaning stations is that an animal, such as a fish or turtle, simply approaches the "station" and signals to a "cleaner fish" that it needs to be cleaned. A cleaner fish will then swim up and remove parasites, not only from the larger animal's skin but also from inside its mouth and gills. Somehow, the larger animal instinctively knows that it has parasites that need to be removed and that there's a place it can go to have smaller fish remove them. The smaller animal knows that it's safe to swim inside the mouth of an animal that's many times its size without the fear of being eaten. This mutually beneficial relationship is neither taught nor learned behavior. It's purely instinctive and truly amazing. This also makes me wonder whether animals can communicate on a level that humans have yet to comprehend. Perhaps they share some type of consciousness-based communication method that is something like a shared understanding.

This example demonstrates the balance that is possible for humanity if we simply learn to work together. Although we don't have cleaning stations, even small, unsolicited acts of kindness toward others, like allowing someone with fewer items to go ahead of you in the supermarket line or holding open a door for the person behind you, can be a good start. I think that we're all innately aware of our potential, but we often become jaded by the challenges of life. Sometimes, it takes a tragedy for us to band together and demonstrate compassion. Maybe this is because it forces us to recognize our vulnerabilities and leads to an enhanced sense of empathy. People seem much more willing to open their hearts when tragedy strikes. Yet in everyday life, we tend to be much more guarded. We tend to be guided more by what we stand to gain and lose.

So, how can our society become a symbiotic ecosystem?

I think that symbiosis starts from inside us and works its way out. After all, it would be difficult to expect that our external environment can be harmonious when we can't even achieve a balance from within. I think this is the key. As I said in the beginning, extreme lifestyles are incredibly difficult to maintain because they require us to make sacrifices to the point of obsession. These obsessions can end up taking the pleasure out of things we used to enjoy. Of course, dedication isn't a bad thing. I am dedicated to many different things, and it's essential for success. There will always be moments when we have to give our complete focus to a particular task—points where the balance may fade—but these moments should be temporary. They should not consume our lives forever. When we become overly entrenched, we start to push others away. This inhibits our ability to interact with others and isolates us. We lose sight of our true priorities.

Maintaining a balanced "internal ecosystem" means that we have to make healthy lifestyle choices. I have been committed to a healthy lifestyle for over a decade. This doesn't mean that I never eat poorly or never have a cocktail. Rather, it means that I try to maintain a balance. There is so much information out there. There are so many diets—so many opinions—that figuring out what works for us can be overwhelming. This might sound cliché, but I think the key is just moderation: from the food we put into our bodies to the information we consume. You just have to research the options and find what works best for you.

I follow a 90/10 diet plan. This means that about 90 percent of the time, I eat very healthy, while I allow myself to indulge the other 10 percent. I find that this stops me from binging and reduces my cravings for crappy food. I also try to listen to my body. When I get a craving for something I normally wouldn't eat, I ask myself whether I'm craving it because my body needs a nutrient provided by it or simply because I feel like indulging. I've also found that living a healthier lifestyle has helped reduce most of the cravings for unhealthy food. This has been even more true with a solid workout regimen. I think twice about eating a slice of pizza once I calculate how much exercise it will take to burn it off. For me, being healthy also means having a healthy routine. This means waking up at 5:30 a.m. every day to work out. I love my morning workouts because they give me energy and help propel me through my day. It's also nice to get it out of the way.

Exercising in the morning is particularly useful when I'm stressed at work. It allows me to focus my energy on releasing the stress as I work out. I try to visualize the stress leaving my body. The harder I push, the more stress I burn off. This is part of the reason I always push myself out of my comfort zone, past the point where my body tells me to quit. I also think that by leaving my comfort zone, I am unlocking my potential for maximum growth. It's when I push myself through the discomfort, fatigue, and mental stress that I feel the best results. I consider it an active form of meditation. I remind myself that the discomfort is only temporary and that I will be rewarded with a healthy body and mind. This also helps me remember that I'm the one in control, not the voice inside my head that tells me to quit. It reminds me that I'm strong. As I'm pushing, I try to remain conscious of how overcoming this challenge translates to every other part of my life. Sometimes the finish line seems so far away but I know that I'll eventually make it. This is true in every aspect of my life.

By keeping a routine, I'm able to maintain a well-balanced internal ecosystem. Sure, it's not always easy. It takes constant effort and motivation. But the harder I work, the sweeter the victory in the end. I remind myself of this daily. A healthy body truly leads to a healthy mind. A healthy mind leads to a positive outlook. A positive outlook leads to more harmonious interactions and relationships with others. This harmony starts from within. After all, we can have all the material success in the world but without our physical and mental health, none of our material success matters. So, although a healthy lifestyle may not ostensibly relate to spirituality, if our internal ecosystems are polluted and worn down, it will be more difficult for us to maintain spiritual alignment. By taking care of our physical vessels, we can keep the body-mind-soul connection balanced and intact.

Using Meditation as Inwardly Focused Prayer

This coincides with the concepts of meditation and prayer. I'm not referring to these ideas in the traditional sense. I honestly don't see the value in reciting words from a book over and over again without actually contemplating the meaning of these words. This is not to say that I don't see a benefit to certain types of prayer; I just think we need to reassess our focus.

This leads me to something I like to refer to as "inwardly focused prayer." This is a type of meditative process through which we focus our positive intentions on a particular outcome. As we will discuss, this inward focus can have demonstrable results in the material world, especially when large groups of people are focused on the same goal. This is a real-world application of the collective consciousness theory. Instead of seeking salvation through some type of external force, we can try to harness our intentions on a positive outcome. Although this type of prayer might seek some type of divine assistance to provide guidance or support in achieving a particular goal, it does not ask for such assistance to complete the task itself. I think that we have far more to gain with this type of prayer than the traditional religious-based approach.

Growing up, my parents forced me to go to Hebrew school. I learned to read Hebrew at an early age and each class would start with at least thirty full minutes of Hebrew prayer. Although I learned to read Hebrew, I was never taught what any of the words meant. I simply recited these meaningless words from a book without having any understanding of what they meant or why I was saying them. We were told only that these were God's rules. I have always felt that my intention matters more than the words I use to express these intentions. I don't even think it's necessary to express these intentions verbally.

This is why I think there's a confluence between prayer and meditation. There has been significant research demonstrating the powerful effect of maintaining a positive and loving state of being, particularly in the group setting. This is because our thoughts are a creative energy force. By directing love and positivity outward, we are cultivating a peaceful and harmonious environment. Likewise, if we can strive to remain in this loving state as often as possible, it will change the nature of our interactions. This is a particularly effective tactic when I'm dealing with someone angry or hostile. Unfortunately, given my profession, this happens far too often. It's not always easy to do, but when I respond to aggression with positivity, my adversaries often find it difficult to remain agitated. I try to embrace the "kill them with kindness" mentality.

Transcendental Meditation and Its Power to Change the World

As I was researching for this book, I stumbled upon a topic that genuinely intrigued me: Transcendental Meditation, or "TM" for short. I was so inspired that I decided to begin my foray into the practice. Although I am admittedly quite new, I have already noticed a demonstrable improvement in the quality of my sleep and generally feel more calm, patient, and focused. As I will explain, unlike other types of mediation I have tried, TM's "go with the flow" (pun intended) approach is exceedingly straightforward and easy to learn. Of course, some sessions are better than others, but overall, it has been a wonderfully rewarding experience, and I would recommend it to anyone.

Even more interesting, over the past few decades, there has been considerable research into the effects of collective meditation on the world at large. The results of this research are truly remarkable and provide real-world evidence of how meditation can have a tangible, quantifiable, and beneficial effect on our society. These studies have focused on the effects of the TM technique, its advanced practice of the TM-Sidhi program, and how this practice can impact large segments of the population, even those who weren't practicing the technique.

I think the spiritual implications of this data are simply far too significant to ignore and align perfectly with the concepts we've discussed in this book. As another testament to synchronicity, I had just finished writing a small section on TM a few days prior when a new colleague of mine brought up the topic of meditation. This prompted a conversation about TM, which, unbeknownst to me, my colleague had been practicing for years. Two days later, he gave me a book called *Strength in Stillness: The Power of Transcendental Meditation* by Bob Roth, a renowned TM instructor who has taught many CEOs and Hollywood elites, including Jerry Seinfeld and Hugh Jackman.

I must admit that I approached the topic skeptically at first. Despite my interest in esoteric subjects, I still approach foreign concepts with a certain degree of skepticism. But the timing of our conversation was simply too perfect to ignore.

The book captivated me immediately. In the opening pages, Roth explains that, unlike other forms of meditation, TM does not require us to push out our thoughts, watch our breath, monitor our sensations, visualize anything, or sit in any particular position. It can be mastered in only a few hours over a few days! TM can be practiced anywhere and requires only twenty minutes twice a day.[80] I meditate at least once a day in my office. This provides me with a much-needed midday respite.

The practice is "simple, natural, and effortless." If you're uncomfortable, you can shift positions. If you're sleepy, then you should allow yourself to fall asleep and start meditating again once you wake up. It requires no concentration or control. It's not a philosophy and requires no lifestyle changes. What's more, TM has absolutely no religious connotations whatsoever. Before I tried TM, I found meditation to be an exercise in futility. My countless attempts had never produced any breakthroughs. But TM is a technique that is astonishingly easy to practice, deeply relaxing, and also incredibly energizing. I think you can see why Roth captured my attention!

The purpose of TM is to open the door to "pure consciousness…a field of limitless creativity, intelligence, and energy within." While Ross stops short of drawing any spiritual analogies in his book, I think the parallels are quite clear: practicing TM can help connect us to both our inner and shared consciousness. TM connects us to the oneness. To use Ross's example, TM allows us to dive beneath the rough waves on the surface of the ocean (our thoughts) into calm depths below (inner stillness).

What I appreciated most about Roth's book is that he doesn't draw support for TM simply by proselytizing. He uses actual scientific and biological data to back up his claims. For example, it's no surprise that stress can shut down our prefrontal cortex. This is the part of the brain responsible for judgment, problem-solving, ethical reasoning, and identity. The amygdala, on the other hand, is the part of the brain that's responsible for emotional responses like our fight-or-flight reflex, which deals with impending crises. When our amygdala is overactivated, we act impulsively and reactively rather than logically. We respond from the fear center. This increases our stress levels, which increases our body's production of cortisol.[81] Increased cortisol levels cause deterioration of otherwise healthy muscle tissue and bone. It also inhibits our body's healing process, weakens the immune system, and has a deleterious effect on digestion, metabolism, and mental function. Increased stress also tends to increase our blood pressure. This, in turn, leads to a greater risk of heart attack and stroke. Several peer-reviewed scientific studies have demonstrated that practicing TM for just a few months correlates with reduced blood pressure and cortisol levels. These studies have also demonstrated a 30 percent reduction in the rate of death from cardiovascular-related causes. This is profoundly significant.

The TM technique was originally founded by Maharishi Mahesh Yogi and was introduced to the West from India in the late 1950s. TM is a systematic technique that is practiced for about twenty minutes twice daily. It requires no effort, beliefs, specific lifestyle, or particular mental abilities.[82] The goal of TM is to allow the individual to experience more silent levels of awareness, which leads to the experience of "pure consciousness," or consciousness without perception or thought. The TM-Sidhi program is an advanced technique that allows for more effective activation of the pure consciousness field and a larger impact on both the individual and society. This idea that energy has a "field" character is exactly what we've been discussing throughout this entire book. It's the premise that there is a fundamental connection underlying all individuals—and all things—through which unity may be achieved and stress may be alleviated at a societal level.

A body of research developed since the late 1970s has demonstrated that the advanced TM-Sidhi program can have some pretty powerful effects when practiced in a group. This research was originally developed to test a prediction made by Maharishi Mahesh Yogi, derived from the Vedic tradition of knowledge, that as little as 1 percent of the total population of a targeted area practicing the advanced TM-Sidhi program twice daily can reduce the stress and create greater harmony on the collective consciousness of the entire population (even those not involved in the TM practice). This theory was later refined to require only as few as the square root of 1 percent of the total targeted population. The square root formula was derived from the study of coherent systems in physics, where the combined intensity of coherent elements is equivalent to the square of the number of elements.

The Vedic tradition underling Maharishi Mahesh Yogi's theory states that the character of pure consciousness one experiences while practicing TM is the universal foundation to the consciousness of every individual. So, the beneficial effects of this experience are shared not only by the individual practicing the technique but also with others. This metaphysical influence on others interacts with the societal level of collective consciousness. This means that the influence of a group practicing TM should measurably affect the largest social unit of which the group is a part, so long as the size of the group exceeds the square root of 1 percent of the population of this social unit.

The practical effect of the square root formula is that it becomes possible to influence very large social units with a very small number of people. For example, a city with one million residents would need a TM-Sidhi group of only one hundred people to have a demonstrable impact. So, at its core, TM is predicated on the understanding that every level of society, from the family level to the world level, has a corresponding collective consciousness. The characteristics of the collective consciousness are the result of the combined qualities of each person's consciousness. For example, if a city's collective consciousness is anxious, it is an amalgam of the experiences and interactions of each of the city's residents. The basic premise of this theory is that because the TM-Sidhi group practice will reduce stress on the collective consciousness, it will consequently reduce stress and violence at the individual level.

This effect has been shown by several published studies, which demonstrated that significant reductions in the rate of violent crime were directly correlated with the creation of TM-Sidhi practitioner groups in which the group's ratio was the square root of 1 percent of the largest population for which there is consistent objective behavioral data available. These were authentic scientific studies that used various scientific methods and took into account a myriad of factors including demographic changes, neighborhood crime detection programs, changes in police coverage, daylight hours, seasonal crime patterns, weather changes, and prior crime trends in both the targeted and neighboring cities.

For example, a 2016 study published by Michael C. Dillbeck and Kenneth L. Cavanaugh (entitled "Societal Violence and Collective Consciousness: Reduction of U.S. Homicide and Urban Violent Crime Rates") reported on the results of an experiment conducted from 2007 to 2010 at the Maharishi International University in Fairfield, Iowa. The study focused on short-term changes in the levels of violent crime and homicides on a national level and utilized students, faculty, staff, and members of the community who convened twice a day to practice the TM and TM-Sidhi program together. The study began when the group exceeded the 1,725 participants needed to represent the square root of 1 percent of the entire United States population, which was estimated to be approximately 297 million people.

The results supported the conclusion that the group practice of the TM-Sidhi program was directly attributed to decreased rates of homicide and violent crime in the United States generally, as well as in a subsample of 206 larger cities between 2007 and 2010. The researchers carefully considered and systematically ruled out alternative hypotheses such as economic changes in the late 2000s and more effective policing strategies. For example, for more effective policing to have contributed to the reduction of homicide and violence in 2007, cities throughout the U.S. would have had to simultaneously implement these strategies. But this wasn't done. So, the geographical confines of the study were simply too wide for any singular factor to be relevant. Significantly, the authors of the study noted that further support for the conclusion that the group practice of the TM-Sidhi program directly attributed to the decline in homicide and violent crime is that this was not the first time this study has been performed. Indeed, the results of the Fairfield study replicated the results of twelve previous peer-reviewed and published studies of this effect.

Taking into account the broader implications of these studies is how they relate to our understanding of collective consciousness. Assuming the results are accurate, it means that we each can transform this planet into a more peaceful and harmonious place with minimal effort and only our minds. If a group of fewer than two thousand people can have such a powerful impact on the entire nation, just imagine what we could achieve with a group of twenty thousand people. Now imagine two hundred thousand people. Now imagine one million people. The possibilities are endless!

CHAPTER 10

PUTTING OUR
SPIRITUALITY TO WORK

Spiritual Evolution Is Cyclical

We have discussed a hodgepodge of spiritual topics. I'd like to close by discussing how the Law of One tackles the idea of spirituality as it relates to our chosen paths: positive versus negative. By choosing to take a spiritual approach to life, we allow ourselves to be more empathetic and understanding people. It makes us more tolerant, patient, loving, and compassionate beings. We begin to recognize our oneness with all other things, and our priorities begin to shift. Despite all of the chaos around us, many of us are waking up to this idea, and our planet is currently undergoing a collective shift toward a more egalitarian society.

According to the Law of One, this shift in consciousness is not merely a coincidence, but rather a product of intelligent design.[83] Indeed, every planet that hosts some type of life-form, be it plant or animal, is at its own stage of spiritual development. These stages of spiritual development are known as "densities," of which there are eight in total. Each planet's density is designed to progress as the spiritual consciousness of the planet evolves. Each density represents an advancement or an increased level of planetary consciousness and spiritual evolution. Our planet could very well be on the verge of a shift in consciousness. I mean, look around. *Something* is happening. It's almost palpable.

Most of us remember the hullabaloo surrounding the end of the Mayan calendar on December 21st, 2012. There was lots of speculation, but nobody witnessed any dramatic changes. The Earth did not explode, aliens didn't land, and the planet just kept on spinning. But from a scientific standpoint, the end of the Mayan calendar marked the end of a 25,920-year cycle. The end of this cycle signifies the point at which the Earth completed a full rotation around the sun and came into a specific geometric alignment with other celestial bodies. Without getting overly technical, using certain geometric configurations, the Mayan calendar can be divided into precisely five equal sections that, when connected, form a pentagon.[84] This approximately 25,900-year cycle was not only recognized by the Mayans and many other ancient civilizations, but it is also recognized by modern science, which refers to this cycle as the "Great Year" or the "Platonic Year."[85] According to NASA, this is the "period of one complete cycle of the equinoxes around the ecliptic." There is substantial scientific evidence that the sun undergoes major energetic shifts at the end of these cycles and these energetic shifts have many effects on our planet including climate changes.[86] So, it's very likely that the Mayan calendar was simply documenting various points at which the Earth is affected by the movement of our sun.

This cycle is related to the Ages of the Zodiac, which uses geometric patterns to divide the sun's 25,900-year orbit into twelve equal and equidistant intervals of 2,160 years, forming a Star of David design. Each 2,160 interval forms a different Age of the Zodiac. If we were to juxtapose the pentagon formation found in the Mayan calendar with the Star of David design formed by the Ages of the Zodiac, they would converge on the very last day of the Great Year. This relates to our discussion because the energetic changes that occur at the end of the 25,900-year cycle—the point at which these two geometrical patterns overlap—have more than just an impact on the Earth itself. The energetic charge we experience at this point is much stronger than what we feel during the rest of the cycle. Because the energy is intelligent by nature and responsible for creating all biological life and DNA, this "grand alignment" could very well have powerful effects on each of us as human beings.

The significance of the 25,920-year cycle is that it represents the point at which humanity will undergo a major energetic shift.

This mean that we could potentially move from third density (the density of awareness) to fourth density (the density of love and understanding). This would also mean that the Mayans and other ancient civilizations understood that not only are these celestial occurrences highly predictable and precise, but they also have very significant spiritual implications. This could indeed be the reason why these civilizations tracked and recorded these anomalies so meticulously in the first place. These events have a direct effect on our individual and planetary spiritual evolution. Unfortunately, I think that religion and science have distorted the significance of this ancient knowledge over time, leaving only a smattering of its remnants like the representation of the Star of David in Judaism. The Law of One reminds us that these cycles and the corresponding density shift are as precise as the striking of a clock on the hour.[87] But this does not mean that our society is prepared to make this transition.

Choosing a Spiritual Path

Whatever your personal beliefs may be, I think we can all agree that humanity has reached a very critical point in its evolution. We are destroying ourselves, each other, and the planet as a whole. I think it's clear that before any real changes can truly occur, we need to learn to live together harmoniously. We need to learn to love others as much as we love ourselves. We need to use this as an opportunity to learn and grow and propel our spiritual evolution into hyperdrive. I think this is a critical juncture in which we all need to make a conscious decision about how we want to live our lives and whether we wish to pursue the positive path or the negative path. On the one hand, the more we align our thoughts and actions with selflessness, the closer we come to the positive path. On the other hand, the more we align our thoughts and actions with selfishness, the closer we come to the negative path. Because energy is at the foundation of everything that exists, is has only two polarities: positive and negative. This is mirrored in our pursuit of spirituality, where we can choose the positive path known as "service to others" or the negative path known as "service to self."[88] Each path presents its own set of challenges and represents a different trajectory of spiritual progression. But both ultimately lead back to oneness with the Creator.

It's important to remember that the terms "positive" and "negative" do not necessarily mean "good" and "evil." Each path is a path of love. Those who choose the positive path focus their love outwardly toward others. Those who choose the negative path focus their love inwardly toward themselves.[89] This means that those who are on the positive path will become more positively oriented, while those who are on the negative path will become more negatively oriented. For example, consider a magnet. A magnet has two distinct polarities: positive and negative. Neither polarity is good or evil. Each serves its own purpose and is necessary for the other to exist. Just as we are unable to judge a magnet's polarity, we are likewise unable to judge the polarity of one's spiritual consciousness. Remember, if all things truly are one, then love and compassion are also one, regardless of whether it is focused inwardly or outwardly.

Consider this choice from a practical perspective. Think about what the world would look like if all of us focused more on being in "service to others"—if each of us began consciously living in the most positive and loving way possible. This is more challenging than it sounds. Life can be very difficult and our society isn't necessarily designed to reward selflessness. It certainly doesn't pay the bills. But being in service to others doesn't mean we need to dedicate our every waking moment to charity at the expense of ourselves and our families. I don't think it's an all-or-nothing proposition. According to the Law of One, there is no singular or best approach.[90] The meaning of service to others is unique to each of us, and only we can decide what it means. The most important thing is that we always remain cognizant of our oneness with the Creator and to all other things.[91]

This means that we don't have to take the concept of service so literally and that it's not our job to "serve" others. We don't have to dedicate our entire lives to charity or forego all of our worldly possessions. It would be very difficult to have a service-to-others mentality if we can't even serve ourselves. If we break this term down to its core, it simply means that we should treat each other with the same unconditional love and compassion that we have for ourselves.[92] This is actually a theme repeated throughout the Bible: "do to others what you would have them do to you."[93] It's that simple. Service to others means that we should strive to see ourselves in others. It means that we should be kind and compassionate and strive to be genuine and honest in our intentions and actions.[94] The more mindful we remain of these goals, the more selfless we become.

We all have the potential to be more positive and loving people. The more we explore our connectedness with the oneness, the more we will recognize our connectedness to those around us. It's the understanding we gain through this introspection that provides us with the greatest potential to serve others. We can even serve others simply by focusing our intentions on being more positive. Indeed, according to the Law of One, when we explore these concepts and focus our intentions, the opportunities to serve others through our everyday experiences becomes limitless.[95] So, we must be introspective and reflect on what service to others means to us. The bottom line is that we are embracing the service-to-others path so long as our thoughts and actions stem from a place of love and compassion.[96]

After reading some of my thoughts on this subject, my editor sent me an article that was originally published in *Scientific American* entitled "What Would Happen If Everyone Truly Believed Everything Is One?" by Scott Barry Kaufman. I was truly blown away when I saw how much overlap there is between the themes of the article and the themes of my book. The author even uses the same Albert Einstein quote that I cited in an earlier chapter! If I'm being honest, when I first read all the overlap, I got very upset. I became paranoid. What if people thought *I* was stealing *his* ideas? But these insecurities quickly dissipated when I realized that this was merely another synchronistic event confirming that not only am I on the right track, but that perhaps my ideas are not as esoteric as I once thought. This is also the perfect example of a situation in which I let my insecurities cloud my logic. Fortunately, I recognized what I was doing and didn't let these thoughts get in the way. I also recognized that the article made some very interesting points that aligned perfectly with what I had been writing about that very day.

The article explores the psychological characteristics of people who have a strong belief in "oneness," the idea that we are all part of some fundamental entity.[97] The article cites several scientific studies demonstrating that a belief in oneness is directly correlated with strong feelings of empathy and compassion. These studies found that people who believe we are all part of the same thing have a significantly more inclusive identity than those who do not. This translates into a greater recognition of our common humanity, our common problems, and—perhaps most importantly—our common imperfections. I think that recognizing our fundamental flaws might be more important than recognizing our fundamental similarities. We are all imperfect people. We are inevitably going to make mistakes. But these mistakes don't necessarily make us bad people.

These studies also found that there was "no relationship between a belief in oneness and the degree to which people endorsed self-focused values" like success and happiness. In other words, the service-to-others values that accompany a belief in oneness are not mutually exclusive with individuality and success. We can have a service-to-others mentality while still maintaining a healthy balance of our own needs. According to the Law of One, to be aligned on the service-to-others path, we need to be only slightly more positively oriented than negatively oriented.[98] This means that we can be a mere 51 percent service to others in our thoughts and actions and still consider ourselves on a positive, service-to-others path. This is not the case with a negatively oriented person, however, as they must approach near totality, attaining a polarity of at least 95 percent negative or service to self.

Practically speaking, this makes sense. Being in service to others focuses our love and compassion outwardly toward others. Since we are all connected, the energy we exchange is preserved, harmonized, and reciprocated.[99] In this sense, by embracing the service-to-others path, we are necessarily being of service to self. Conversely, the negative or service-to-self path is unsustainable and will ultimately break down as a result of spiritual entropy. This is because the service-to-self path inherently results in power and dominion over others, which causes the energy to weaken and eventually disintegrate. In the end, those who are on a negative path will ultimately (over many lifetimes) have to change course and pursue a positive path. So, neither choice is right or wrong; however, to have a more caring, compassionate, and loving planet we must collectively choose the positive path. Our struggle as a society in making this choice is timeless and is where religion intersects with spirituality.

The Law of One says that the most important decision we make as third-density beings is whether to pursue the positive path or the negative path.[100] The very purpose of third density is to provide a foundation for this choice. This isn't necessarily a conscious decision that occurs during a single lifetime, but rather a product of our decisions over many incarnations. Of course, by consciously making decisions that align with a particular path, we can make this happen faster. This "choice" occurs once we become either 51 percent positive (service to others) or 95 percent negative (service to self). Once we reach these levels in third density, we have officially chosen a path and have gained enough polarity to move through subsequent densities. At this point, we are then ready to move to fourth density, which is the density of love and understanding. This is where we begin to refine our choice by focusing our love either outwardly (those on the service-to-others path) or inwardly (those on the service-to-self path).

May the Force Be with You

As strange as this concept may seem, humanity's struggle between the positive and the negative paths is the basis of many of the best and most entertaining literature and films. Let's take Star Wars as an example. Upon closer examination, it's very clear to me that George Lucas understood the spiritual significance of this choice and made this the underlying theme of the film. The original three movies are all about guiding Luke Skywalker toward a choice: the "light side" or the "dark side" of this concept called the "Force." The Force is explained throughout the movies as a mysterious field of energy created by life that binds the universe together.[101] The Jedi (the good guys) and the Sith (the bad guys) both derive extraordinary power from the Force, including telekinesis, extrasensory perception (ESP), and clairvoyance. Obi-Wan Kenobi, one of the movies' main characters, describes the Force as "an energy field created by all living things. It surrounds us and penetrates us; it binds the galaxy together."[102] This sounds a whole lot like the concepts explained in the Law of One, doesn't it?

What's more, the Force has two polarities: the light side and the dark side. The light side of the Force is aligned with unconditional love and supports honesty, empathy, and compassion. The dark side of the Force, on the other hand, is considered more seductive and is aligned with emotions such as fear, anger, and hatred. The Jedi derive their powers from the light side of the Force and serve as guardians of the peace and justice. The Jedi use the Force only for knowledge and defense, but never to attack.[103] The Sith are the Jedi's mortal enemies and derive their powers from the dark side of the Force. The Sith exploit the Force to manipulate and hurt others and are obsessed with amassing power regardless of the consequences. Yoda, perhaps the oldest and most powerful Jedi, explains that although the dark side is quicker, easier, and more seductive, it is not stronger.

There is a pivotal scene in *Return of the Jedi* when Darth Vader faces off with Luke Skywalker (his son) while the powerful Sith Emperor Palpatine watches. Darth Vader tells Luke that the only way to save himself and his loved ones is to give in to the dark side, but Luke refuses. Luke then attacks Darth Vader, severing Darth Vader's hand in the process. Instead of being upset, the Emperor is excited by this turn of events and tells Luke that he must fulfill his destiny by joining the dark side. In an act of pure martyrdom, Luke drops his weapon and says, "Never. I'll never turn to the dark side."[104] Just as the Emperor is about to kill Luke, Darth Vader, in a surprising final act of valor, saves Luke by killing the Emperor. As Darth Vader lies dying, he asks Luke to remove his helmet (the only thing keeping him alive) so that he can finally look at him with his own eyes. At this moment, it's clear that Darth Vader has returned to the light side and that love will always conquer hate.

Think about the spiritual implications of this scene. Luke's commitment to the light side, even in the face of imminent death, not only gave him the power to defeat Darth Vader, one of the most powerful Sith lords the galaxy has ever known, but it also inspired this same Sith lord, the absolute epitome of darkness, to choose love over hate. This shows the power of the positive path.

This is very similar to *Harry Potter*, which is another classic light-versus-dark story. Here, too, there is a critical apex where light and dark meet. Harry Potter is forced to face off against one of the most powerful dark wizards of all time, Voldemort. Yet Harry, even when faced with near-certain death, refuses to succumb to darkness. In the epic showdown, Voldemort fires a death spell at Harry with his wand. Harry, rather than responding with a death spell of his own, simply returns fire with one of the most basic and benevolent spells of all, seeking to do nothing more than disarm his opponent. Ironically, Harry's benign maneuver causes Voldemort's death spell to backfire, killing him instantly. Harry had defeated the most powerful and feared wizard of all time without ever succumbing to the darkness of violence. This is an incredibly powerful message.

My Spiritual Journey

As I said in the beginning, this is not a step-by-step guide to how spirituality can change your life. I find the subject fascinating and enjoy the philosophical explorations that come along with it. I don't have a clear-cut answer for how spirituality has changed my life, nor do I have a foolproof system for how you can achieve your own spiritual growth. I can say that being a spiritual person has certainly helped shape my perspective on life and how I approach difficult situations. It has made me a more calm, peaceful, and loving person. I ask myself whether I'm living my truth, whether I'm acting in service to others, and whether I'm taking steps to accomplish what I set out to achieve. I remain mindful of my priorities so that I never lose sight of my goals.

Being spiritual has also helped me identify my real priorities and not get bogged down by my ego-driven emotions. This can be difficult, especially because I've always had to work incredibly hard for everything I have. Nothing has been handed to me. But I refuse to allow myself to embody a victim's mentality. This can only create blame. Blame leads to anger; anger leads to resentment. It becomes a cycle. Allowing myself to get caught in this type of cycle will only hinder my spiritual progress. I would be searching for blame instead of seeking solutions. Solutions lead to outcomes, whereas blame only leads to stagnation. This, too, requires balance, and I often have to remind myself that success and selfishness are not synonymous and that I have to balance my own happiness with the happiness of others. I also have to remind myself that it's okay to let loose and have a little fun. Life can't be all serious all the time.

Of course, I still become stressed and angry at times, but I try to remain mindful that all things—every encounter, every word I speak—are necessary parts of my spiritual evolution. I try to remind myself daily that all of my actions have a universal effect. The key for me to dealing with these emotions is to recognize how I'm feeling, why I feel that way, and to let go of the negativity as quickly as possible. This is not always easy. Life can sometimes be agonizingly stressful, and I'd be lying if I said there are never times when I lose control and let the stress overcome my rationality. I'd also be lying if I said there are never times when I question my purpose or beliefs. But I try to remind myself that in the grand scheme of existence, my problems are relatively minimal. Holding onto the stress and anxiety only clouds my clarity and inhibits my growth. Obsessing over the hypothetical "what ifs" does nothing but distract me from my goals. Nor does it give me any satisfaction. I still plan for contingencies, but I try not to let these possibilities take precedence over my goals.

Besides, it's through the struggles and adversity that I have become the person I am today. Every one of my struggles has made me a stronger person and taught me a valuable lesson, and it's through these lessons that I've learned the most. Heck, the reason I wrote this book is because of these very struggles. Understanding this hasn't necessarily made the struggles in my life any easier, but it's certainly made them more manageable. It's given me perspective and helped me become a more pragmatic and proactive person. The true test comes after I've had a particularly stressful day and am able to stay calm by reminding myself that I'll eventually find a solution to whatever problem

I'm having. Even when the problem seems insurmountable and the solution isn't clear, I know that I'll find a way. I always do and I always will. This has been true throughout all of my adult life. For example, prior to graduating law school, while everyone was freaking out about finding a job, I remained calm. I knew that opportunities would present themselves so long as I was positive and proactive. Surely enough, one of my professors reached out to me completely unsolicited about a legal fellowship opportunity within his department. I had no idea this position even existed until he contacted me. But it was an amazing opportunity and helped me secure a lot of great connections, one of which led directly to my next job.

Staying mindful of my oneness also helps keep me grounded. I encourage conversations with as many people as possible because I think these human interactions are rewarding and insightful. I try to treat each and every person I encounter with the respect and dignity they deserve. This keeps me humble and it keeps me human. But it's also necessary to find a balance, which can sometimes be difficult. Identifying our boundaries can also be challenging. Although I always try to help others whenever I can, I've had to learn when I need to put my foot down and say no so that people don't mistake my kindness for weakness. There's a fine line between being generous and allowing someone to take advantage of my generosity. From a karmic perspective, if I allow people to take advantage of me, then I have only myself to blame and it will keep happening until I learn. It took me many years to recognize this line and it's something I'm still learning to identify. Learning to trust and follow my instincts has been an important part of this process. In retrospect, there were many unpleasant situations I could have avoided had I simply listened to my instincts. Forcing myself to slow down, step back, and objectively assess a situation has been critical in this learning experience. As cliché as this sounds, I really, truly try to focus on living in the moment. By remaining positive, I attract more positivity into my life, including other like-minded people.

Overall, my experiences, and particularly my struggles, have fueled my ambition to succeed so that I can not only provide for myself, but also help others along the way. I feel that material success is pointless if I have nobody to share it with. Perhaps it was my unique upbringing that reinforced my innate desire to help others. This desire has solidified and galvanized my sense of spirituality and purpose. This sense of purpose is what guided me through law school and has kept me honest in my quest for spiritual fulfillment in my career. This quest is what has inspired me to write this book and encouraged me to finish. There were certainly many moments when I felt like I was wasting my time and that nobody cares what I have to say. But I pushed through these feelings and reminded myself that even if this book never sells a single copy, writing it was an essential part of my spiritual and creative development. As frustrating as this process has been at times, I have always remained focused on the end product, visualizing myself crossing the finish line as I make the very final edit to my manuscript. It's a truly remarkable feeling, and the sense of fulfillment this has brought me is unparalleled.

Every day presents a new set of challenges, some easier than others. But I have learned that my outlook has a fairly significant impact on the outcome of these challenges. Having a positive outlook tends to result in more positive outcomes, even if it's not the specific outcome I had hoped. But that's why I try to remain positive in every situation, especially the most difficult ones. I ask myself what the experience can teach me and how I can improve. Even as I write these very words, I'm not quite certain what to expect from this book, but I know that it's part of my spiritual journey and hope that it inspires more people to pursue their own personal truth. It's also helped me realize how much I enjoy writing and talking about this topic. Nothing keeps me more present than being immersed in spirituality. I find it energizing and invigorating. Writing this book has also made me recognize that I need to incorporate my spirituality into my career.

I don't think I can ever truly be happy unless I'm doing something that makes me feel fulfilled, and I won't be fulfilled unless I'm doing work that truly makes a difference in people's lives in one way or another. This doesn't mean that I need to go off the grid and join the Peace Corps. It just means that I'm going to continue pursuing a path that allows me to embody the true virtues of my profession, as both a counselor and attorney-at-law. I think that far too many people in the legal field have forgotten that being a lawyer doesn't just mean advocating or arguing or negotiating for our clients, it also requires a great deal of counseling, both legal and psychological. Counseling is the part of the job I love the most. I sort of like the sound of that: Spiritual Counsel and Attorney-at-Law. Maybe I'll even put that on my business cards!

I genuinely hope this book provided you with a refreshing and unique perspective on spirituality. I hope that you feel inspired to continue your spiritual pursuits and to make spirituality a more prominent focus in your everyday life. I hope that you feel impassioned to discover and speak your truth. I hope that you feel empowered to discuss your beliefs—not only about spirituality but about everything—more openly and honestly with your peers. I hope you recognize the great power that you possess to make positive changes both on an individual and on a collective level. And I hope that this book is merely the beginning of your lifelong endeavor toward introspection, investigation, discovery, and growth.

It has been a great honor and privilege to share this information with you. Indeed, as the Law of One reminds us, "we are [each] truly humble messengers of the Law of One" and "we encourage a dispassionate attempt to share information without concern for numbers or quick growth among others. That you attempt to make this information available is, in your term, your service. *The attempt, if it reaches one, reaches all.*[105]

So, liberate yourself. Be who you are meant to be. And above all, *live* your truth, whatever that may be.

ENDNOTES

1. "What Is Metaphysics?" *University of Sedona*. 13 Sept. 2019, universityofsedona.com/meaning-of-metaphysics/.

2. "The Law of One (The Ra Material)." *The Law of One*, www.lawofone.info/.

3. Wilcock, David. *The Synchronicity Key: The Hidden Intelligence Guiding the Universe and You*. Dutton, 2016.

4. "The Law of One Session 1, Question 1." *The Law of One*, https://www.lawofone.info/s/1.

5. Wilcock, David. *The Synchronicity Key: The Hidden Intelligence Guiding the Universe and You*. Dutton, 2016.

6. "The Law of One (The Ra Material)." *The Law of One*, www.lawofone.info/.

7. "The Law of One Session 50, Question 7." *The Law of One*, https://www.lawofone.info/s/50#7.

8. "The Law of One Session 1, Question 6." *The Law of One*, https://www.lawofone.info/s/1#6.

9. Jung, Carl G. *Archetypes and the Collective Unconscious*. Routledge, 2014.

10. Jung, Carl G. *The Structure and Dynamics of the Psyche*. Pantheon Books, 1960.

11. Jung, Carl G. *The Structure and Dynamics of the Psyche*. Pantheon Books, 1960.

12. Jung, Carl G. *Man and His Symbols*. Doubleday, 1972.

13. Cowell, Alan. "After 350 Years, Vatican Says Galileo Was Right: It Moves." *The New York Times*. 31 Oct. 1992, www.nytimes.com/1992/10/31/world/after-350-years-vatican-says-galileo-was-right-it-moves.html.

14. "The Law of One Session 1." *The Law of One,* https://www.lawofone.info/s/1.

15. Moskowitz, Clara. "Fact or Fiction?: Energy Can Neither Be Created Nor Destroyed." *Scientific American*. 5 Aug. 2014. www.scientificamerican.com/article/energy-can-neither-be-created-nor-destroyed/.

16. "E = mc2 Explained." *NOVA*. Aug. 2005. www.pbs.org/wgbh/nova/einstein/lrk-hand-emc2expl.html.

17. Carroll, Joshua. "A Fun Way of Understanding E=mc2." *Universe Today*. 23 Dec. 2015. www.universetoday.com/114617/a-fun-way-of-understanding-emc2/.

18. "E = mc2 Explained." *NOVA*. Aug. 2005. www.pbs.org/wgbh/nova/einstein/lrk-hand-emc2expl.html.

19. "The Law of One Session 13, Question 6." *The Law of One,* https://www.lawofone.info/s/13#6.

20. "Interview with Dalai Lama." *Buddhism Now,* vol. III, no. 4, 1991.

21. Einstein, Albert. "Letter to Robert S. Marcus." Received by Robert S. Marcus. 12 Feb. 1950.

22. Coolman, Robert. "What Is Quantum Mechanics?" *Live Science*. 26 Sept. 2014. www.livescience.com/33816-quantum-mechanics-explanation.html.

23. Bennett, Jay. "The Double-Slit Experiment That Blew Open Quantum Mechanics." 28 July 2016, www.popularmechanics.com/science/a22094/video-explainer-double-slit-experiment/.

24. Thompson, Avery. "The Logic-Defying Double-Slit Experiment Is Even Weirder Than You Thought." *Popular Mechanics*. 1 Aug. 2016. www.popularmechanics.com/science/a22280/double-slit-experiment-even-weirder/.

25. Williams, Matt. "What Is the Double Slit Experiment?" *Universe Today,* 18 Jan 2011. www.universetoday.com/83380/double-slit-experiment/.

26. Bennett, Jay. "The Double-Slit Experiment That Blew Open Quantum Mechanics." 28 July 2016. www.popularmechanics.com/science/a22094/video-explainer-double-slit-experiment/.

27. Ball, Philip. "The Strange Link between the Human Mind and Quantum Physics." *BBC.* 16 Feb. 2017. www.bbc.com/earth/story/20170215-the-strange-link-between-the-human-mind-and-quantum-physics.

28. "The Law of One Session 28, Question 1." *The Law of One*, www.lawofone.info/s/28#1.

29. "Interview with Dalai Lama." *Buddhism Now,* vol. III, no. 4, 1991.

30. "The Law of One Session 27, Question 5." *The Law of One*, www.lawofone.info/s/28#5.

31. Potential Energy." *The Physics Classroom.* www.physicsclassroom.com/class/energy/Lesson-1/Potential-Energy.

32. "The Law of One Session 27, Question 5." *The Law of One*, www.lawofone.info/s/28#5.

33. "The Law of One Session 82, Question 10." *The Law of One*, www.lawofone.info/s/82#10.

34. "The Law of One Session 13, Question 5." *The Law of One*, www.lawofone.info/s/13#5.

35. "The Law of One Session 13, Question 6." *The Law of One*, www.lawofone.info/s/13#6.

36. "The Law of One Session 13, Question 7." *The Law of One*, www.lawofone.info/s/13#7.

37. "The Law of One Session 27, Questions 6-7." *The Law of One*, www.lawofone.info/s/27#6.

38. "The Law of One Session 4, Question 20." *The Law of One*, www.lawofone.info/s/4#20.

39. "Big Bang Theory." AllAboutScience.org. www.big-bang-theory.com/.

40. "The Law of One Session 13, Question 12." *The Law of One*, www.lawofone.info/s/13#12.

41. Wilcock, David. *The Synchronicity Key: The Hidden Intelligence Guiding the Universe and You.* Dutton, 2016.

42. "The Law of One Session 78, Question 9." *The Law of One*, www.lawofone.info/s/78#9.

43. "The Law of One Session 13, Question 8." *The Law of One*, www.lawofone.info/s/13#8.

44. "The Law of One Session 78, Question 9." *The Law of One*, www.lawofone.info/s/78#9.

45. "The Law of One Session 13, Questions 8-9." *The Law of One*, www. lawofone.info/s/13#8.

46. "The Law of One Session 13, Question 8." *The Law of One*, www. lawofone.info/s/13#8.

47. "The Law of One Session 13, Questions 8-9." *The Law of One*, www. lawofone.info/s/13#8.

48. "The Law of One Session 13, Questions 8-13." *The Law of One*, www. lawofone.info/s/13#8.

49. Beall, Abigail. "Theory Claims to Offer the First 'Evidence' Our Universe Is a Hologram." *WIRED UK*. 31 Jan. 2017. www.wired.co.uk/ article/our-universe-is-a-hologram.

50. Wilcock, David. *The Synchronicity Key: The Hidden Intelligence Guiding the Universe and You*. Dutton, 2016.

51. Wall, Mike. "The Universe Has Probably Hosted Many Alien Civilizations: Study." *Space.com*. 5 May 2016. www.space.com/32793-intelligent-alien-life-probability-high.html.

52. Rosenberg, Eli. "Former Navy Pilot Describes UFO Encounter Studied by Secret Pentagon Program." *The Washington Post*. 18 Dec. 2017, www. washingtonpost.com/amphtml/news/checkpoint/wp/2017/12/18/ former-navy-pilot-describes-encounter-with-ufo-studied-by-secret-pentagon-program/.

53. Weisberger, Mindy. "Pentagon's Secret, Defunct UFO-Hunting Program May Still Exist." *LiveScience*. 28 July 2020. www.livescience. com/pentagon-ufo-agency-still-active.html.

54. Altman, Howard, and J.D. Simkins. "Pentagon Creates UFO Task Force to See If Aerial Objects Pose Threat." *Military Times*. 14 Aug. 2020. www.militarytimes.com/news/your-military/2020/08/14/pentagon-creates-ufo-task-force-to-see-if-unidentified-aerial-phenomena-pose-threat/.

55. "Pentagon Just Admitted to 'Testing' UFO Wreckage. But What Did They Discover?" *MSN*. 16 Feb 2021. https://www.msn.com/en-in/ news/world/the-pentagon-just-admitted-to-testing-ufo-wreckage-heres-what-they-have-discovered/ar-BB1dHhnQ

56. Reich, Aaron. "Former Israeli Space Security Chief Says Aliens Exist, Humanity Not Ready." *The Jerusalem Post*. 10 Dec 2020. https://m-jpost-com.cdn.ampproject.org/c/s/m.jpost.com/omg/former-israeli-space-security-chief-says-aliens-exist-humanity-not-ready-651405/amp.

57. *Ibid.*

216

58. *Ibid.*

59. *Ibid.*

60. *Ibid.*

61. Wilcock, David. *The Synchronicity Key: The Hidden Intelligence Guiding the Universe and You.* Dutton, 2016.

62. "Sri Chakra Research." *Google Sites,* sites.google.com/site/ srichakraresearch/.

63. Sodini, Jennifer. "Mysterious 13-Mile-Long Sri Yantra Mandala Crop Circle Found in Desert." *NewEarth Media,* 5 Feb. 2016, newearth. media/mysterious-13-mile-long-sri-yanta-mandala-crop-circle-found-in-desert/.

64. Joshi, Risha. "The Pineal Gland & Symbol of Manifestation - The Sri Yantra." *PowerThoughts Meditation Club,* 29 Sept. 2016, powerthoughtsmeditationclub.com/the-pineal-gland-symbol-of-manifestation-the-sri-yantra/.; "What Is the Sri Yantra?" *Crystal Dreams World,* 5 Oct. 2020, crystaldreamsworld.com/what-is-the-sri-yantra/.

65. Joshi, Risha. "The Pineal Gland & Symbol of Manifestation - The Sri Yantra." *PowerThoughts Meditation Club.* 31 Aug. 2015. powerthoughtsmeditationclub.com/the-pineal-gland-symbol-of-manifestation-the-sri-yantra/.

66. "What Is the Sri Yantra?" *Crystal Dreams World.* 5 Oct. 2020. crystaldreamsworld.com/what-is-the-sri-yantra/.

67. "Opinion." *Dictionary.com.* www.dictionary.com/browse/opinion?s=t.

68. Wamsley, Laurel. "Bill Maher Apologizes After Using N-Word On His Show." *NPR.* 3 June 2017. www.npr.org/sections/thetwo-way/2017/06/03/531365550/bill-maher-apologizes-after-using-n-word-on-his-show.

69. "TV's Roseanne Says Tweet 'Cost Me Everything' but Wasn't Racist." *CNBC.* 27 July 2018. www.cnbc.com/2018/07/27/tvs-roseanne-says-tweet-cost-me-everything-but-wasnt-racist.html.

70. "The Law of One Session 34, Question 5." *The Law of One,* www. lawofone.info/s/34#5.

71. "Newton's Third Law of Motion." *The Physics Classroom,* www. physicsclassroom.com/class/newtlaws/Lesson-4/Newton-s-Third-Law.

72. "The Law of One Session 34, Question 5." *The Law of One,* www. lawofone.info/s/34#5.

73. "The Law of One Session 18, Question 12." *The Law of One,* http:// www.lawofone.info/s/18#12.

74. "The Law of One Session 34, Question 5." *The Law of One*, www.lawofone.info/s/34#5.

75. "The Law of One Session 18, Question 12." *The Law of One*, http://www.lawofone.info/s/18#12.

76. "The Law of One Session 21, Question 9." *The Law of One*, http://www.lawofone.info/s/21#9.

77. Weiss, Brian L. *Many Lives, Many Masters: The True Story of a Prominent Psychiatrist, His Young Patient, and Past-Life Therapy That Changed Both Their Lives*. Fireside, 1988.

78. Jung, Carl G. *Synchronicity: An Acausal Connecting Principle*. Pantheon Books, 1955.

79. "Cleaning Station." *Wikipedia*, Wikimedia Foundation, 30 Mar. 2020. en.wikipedia.org/wiki/Cleaning_station.

80. Roth, Robert. *Strength in Stillness: The Power of Transcendental Meditation*. Simon and Schuster, 2018.

81. Roth, Robert. *Strength in Stillness: The Power of Transcendental Meditation*. Simon and Schuster, 2018.

82. Cavanaugh, Kenneth L., and Michael C. Dillbeck. "Societal Violence and Collective Consciousness: Reduction of U.S. Homicide and Urban Violent Crime Rates." *SAGE Journals*, 14 Apr. 2016, journals.sagepub.com/doi/full/10.1177/2158244016637891.

83. "The Law of One Session 28, Question 15." *The Law of One*, http://www.lawofone.info/s/28#15.; "The Law of One Session 16, Question 51." *The Law of One*, http://www.lawofone.info/s/16#51.

84. Wilcock, David. *The Synchronicity Key: The Hidden Intelligence Guiding the Universe and You*. Dutton, 2016.

85. "Dictionary of Technical Terms for Aerospace Use - G." *NASA*. er.jsc.nasa.gov/seh/g.html.

86. Wilcock, David. *The Synchronicity Key: The Hidden Intelligence Guiding the Universe and You*. Dutton, 2016.

87. "The Law of One Session 13, Question 23." *The Law of One*, http://www.lawofone.info/s/13#23.

88. "The Law of One Session 76, Question 16." *The Law of One*, http://www.lawofone.info/s/76#16.

89. "The Law of One Session 48, Question 6." *The Law of One*, http://www.lawofone.info/s/48#6.

90. "The Law of One Session 17, Question 30." *The Law of One*, http://www.lawofone.info/s/17#30.

91. "The Law of One Session 15, Question 7." *The Law of One*, http://www.lawofone.info/s/15#7.

92. "The Law of One Session 17, Question 30." *The Law of One*, http://www.lawofone.info/s/17#30.

93. "Matthew 7:12." *Bible Gateway*, www.biblegateway.com/passage/?search=Matthew+7%3A12&version=NIV.; "Luke 6:31." *Bible Gateway*, www.biblegateway.com/passage/?search=Luke+6%3A31&version=NIV.

94. "The Law of One Session 17, Question 30." *The Law of One*, http://www.lawofone.info/s/17#30.

95. "The Law of One Session 15, Question 7." *The Law of One*, http://www.lawofone.info/s/15#7.

96. "The Law of One Session 17, Question 30." *The Law of One*, http://www.lawofone.info/s/17#30.

97. Kaufman, Scott Barry. "What Would Happen If Everyone Truly Believed Everything Is One?" *Scientific American Blog Network*, Scientific American, 8 Oct. 2018, blogs.scientificamerican.com/beautiful-minds/what-would-happen-if-everyone-truly-believed-everything-is-one/.

98. "The Law of One Session 17, Question 31." *The Law of One*, http://www.lawofone.info/s/17#31.

99. "The Law of One Session 7, Question 15." *The Law of One*, http://www.lawofone.info/s/7#15.

100. "The Law of One Session 76, Question 16." *The Law of One*, http://www.lawofone.info/s/76#16.

101. "The Force." *StarWars.com*, www.starwars.com/databank/the-force.

102. "The Force." *Wikipedia*, Wikimedia Foundation, 29 Jan. 2021, en.wikipedia.org/wiki/The_Force.

103. "Star Wars: Episode V - The Empire Strikes Back." *Star Wars: Episode V - The Empire Strikes Back Quotes*, www.quotes.net/movies/star_wars:_episode_v_-_the_empire_strikes_back_10918.

104. *Return of the Jedi*. Directed by Richard Marquand. Twentieth Century Fox, 1983.

105. "The Law of One Session 28, Question 17." *The Law of One*, http://www.lawofone.info/s/28#17.